The Beginner's Ancestor Research Kit

Philip Breck
with
Frederick Van Hon Garretson

BRISTOL PUBLISHING ENTERPRISES, INC.
San Leandro, California

Printed in the United States of America.

ISBN 1-55867-019-X

Cover design: Frank Paredes
Graphic design: Leslie Foley

TABLE OF CONTENTS

THE AUTHORS

The late Philip Breck was an active genealogist for 20 years, and a member of national and local genealogical societies in the United States, England and Scotland. Prior to founding his own management and public relations firm in 1953, he was a Chamber of Commerce manager, bank officer and World War II naval officer. Breck was a graduate of the University of California.

The late Frederick Van Hon Garretson coauthored the original manuscript. He was an Oakland, California newspaperman who was the recipient of numerous journalism awards for coverage of news of national resources and the environment. He did extensive genealogical research throughout the United States, England and Ireland.

INTRODUCTION

You are about to embark in your own personal time capsule on a trip back into history to meet people who have had more influence on your life than any others: your ancestors.

You may discover that you are descended from William the Conqueror, but more probably you will find that you are descended from a village blacksmith in a small town of which you have never heard. Sooner or later curiosity will compel you to visit your ancestor's town and there you will discover relatives you didn't know existed. You will like some of your new-found relatives and detest others, but you will have discovered a great deal about yourself.

Traditionally, American genealogy has been concerned with tracing descent from an immigrant ancestor, or, hopefully, finding that one is an heir to a great fortune or descended from a famous personality! These things happen, but the real value of genealogy (which Webster defines as "a history of the descent of a person or a family from an ancestor") is finding out about the genes and environments which have gone into making you what you are.

This kit contains all of the forms and instructions you need to prepare a simple family history, beginning with you, your children or grandchildren, and going back four or five generations on both male and female lines. It is based on sound professional practices in the field of genealogy, but it is deliberately simple. It omits many complex methods involved in proving relationships that are not clearly established by personal knowledge or by birth, marriage and death certificates. The pages are three-hole punched and perforated to put into a three-ring binder.

This introduction to family research, if followed step by step, will give you all the "know-how" you need until you run into complicated problems, and it tells you how to get help in solving those problems.

You may use this system to extend your family history back 1,000 years. You have permission to photocopy as many more forms as you wish.

HOW TO BEGIN

The Genealogical Chart

The first step in preparing your family history is to complete the enclosed genealogical charts as far back as your knowledge of your family permits. Instructions for completing these charts are set forth on pages 3 and 4. If you trace your family back more than twelve generations, you will need a numbering system adapted to your own specific needs, but by that time you will have read enough genealogies, seen enough different sorts of genealogical charts and learned enough about genealogical research to "do your own thing."

The Ancestor Chart

Now make up your ancestor charts (you have enough forms to prepare a record for each name on Genealogical Chart #1). *Be sure to list your sources.* If you haven't enough room on the printed side, make entries on the reverse side. These ancestor charts can either be placed in your notebook following the genealogical chart on which the names of the ancestors appear, can be kept in a separate notebook in alphabetic order, or may be placed in a file prepared for each surname. (Or you may find it more convenient to put this information on 3-x-5-inch index cards.)

Visit, phone or write to relatives who may have additional information. Make a special effort to fill in every possible detail on these record sheets. If birth dates are not available, try to rank the children from oldest to youngest.

Your Notebook

Buy some 8½-x-11-inch composition paper and insert it into the three-ring binder you have acquired for your genealogical charts. Carry this with you whenever you interview a relative, visit a genealogical library, tour a cemetery or snoop in public records at a county courthouse. Don't be afraid to make many notes; all too often you will not remember very simple facts unless you write them down.

Family Records

At this point you will have already discovered how little you really know about your ancestors, so get some file folders (letter- or legal-size — there are advantages and disadvantages to each) and label a separate file with each surname appearing on your genealogical chart. Put into these folders all original (or copies of) family records you can find, being sure you list where and/or from whom you got them.

Whenever possible, make a photocopy of source material and put it in your file. Most libraries and public archives now have relatively inexpensive copying equipment available for your use in making copies. Copy the title page of books for convenient future reference.

Family Photographs

Family photo albums are a rich source of family information. Try to make copies of old photographs and store them in a separate place. In the event of a tragic accident or fire, you may save the only surviving photograph of a long dead ancestor.

Identify all the people in each pho-

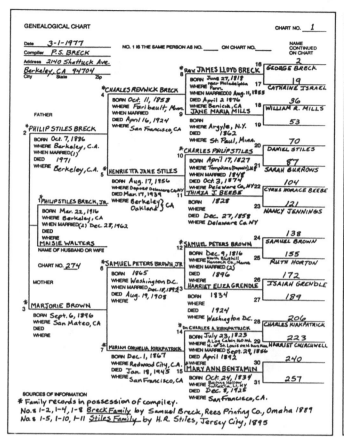

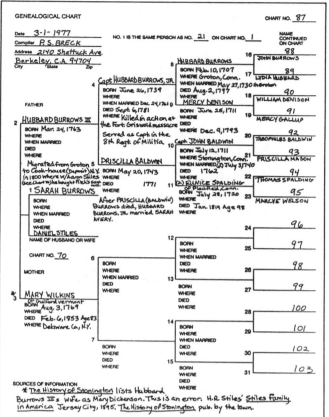

CHARTS NUMBERED BY THE BRECK SYSTEM

tograph. Write down their names, relationships and the date on the back of each picture with a soft pencil.

At this point you have already compiled a family history. How detailed you make it is up to you.

PREPARING YOUR GENEALOGICAL CHART

The first step in compiling your family history is to decide on a point of beginning: the person who will be Number 1 on Chart #1. It could be yourself, your spouse, your parent, your child (or niece or nephew), your grandchild, your great-grandchild or anyone else whose ancestry you wish to record.

Enter the beginning name as #1 on a blank genealogical chart removed from the back of this instruction manual and inserted in your notebook. List his or her father and mother in blanks #2 and #3 and so on until you come to the fifth column, #16 to #31. Ancestors #16 to #31 on all charts are ancestor #1 on a continuation chart.

Under *sources of information* at the bottom of each genealogical chart *list*

3

each source from which you derived information. It may not seem important to you now, but take our word for it: you will soon have so much data that you will forget where you got particular pieces of information unless you write down the sources.

NUMBERING GENEALOGICAL CHARTS

One of the most perplexing problems a starting genealogist faces is, "How do you number the charts?" when you have several lines going back more than five generations. There is no "best method" or "standard method." Use whatever best fits your needs. You may want to devise your own system.

The Breck System

The numbering system shown on the charts in this genealogical primer produces a twelve-generation genealogy on 273 consecutively numbered pedigree charts. Pages 1, 2 and 3 will be ancestors with your surname. This basic system directly encompasses only the 4,095 ancestors a person may have in twelve generations, but with minor modifications (prefixing a letter of the alphabet and starting a whole new series of charts), it can be expanded backwards for an infinite number of generations. A major advantage of the Breck System is that the numbers of charts never contain more than four digits plus a letter or combination of letters.

A Basic System

If you don't like the Breck System, a simple system you might try temporarily, while looking for something better, is to pick up the numbers on the enclosed pedigree charts. Your paternal great-great-grandfather's name is written on the line after the number 16, so his ancestors would be on Chart #16. The next chart on that paternal line (generations 9 through 13) would be on #16-16 and so on. While this looks like a blur of numbers, one can quickly find which chart attaches where.

A Pyramid System

Another system, used by many professionals, is based on the pyramid of numbers seen on the chart of Winston Churchill's ancestry (page 5). Each person has a specific "ancestor number" which is useful for filing purposes. Males have even numbers and females odd. Double a person's number and you get the father's ancestor number, add one and you have the mother's number. The ancestor numbers can be used as chart numbers when you jump from one chart to the next. The numbers extend back infinitely.

For example, using these instructions, number each person on the lineages of President Gerald Ford and President Richard Nixon (shown on page 12). You'll find that Rev. Stephen Bachiler is Ford's ancestor #14,738 and Nixon's #3,394. This system is universal and can be used to chart any kind of pedigree — race horses or royalty, a dog or a duke.

THE AMERICAN ANCESTRY OF SIR WINSTON CHURCHILL 1874-1965, THROUGH HIS MOTHER JENNIE JEROME, 1854-1921, WHO IN 1874 MARRIED LORD RANDOLPH CHURCHILL, SECOND SON OF THE DUKE OF MARLBOROUGH

The American ancestry of Sir Winston Churchill is depicted here on a standard nine-generation pedigree chart which has space on the back to extend a few lineages back fifteen generations. Only a portion of the back side is reproduced here.

Blank copies of the fifteen-generation chart (copyrighted by Grant L. Misback) measure 25 by 27 inches and are distributed by Bookcraft, Inc., of Salt Lake City, Utah.

Data on the chart is adapted from articles by Conklin Mann in the New York Genealogical and Biographical Record, vol. 73, No. 3; July 1942. Indian ancestry is from Ralph G. Martin's *Jennie - The Life of Lady Randolph Churchill,* vol. 1, pp. 15, 323, 324.

However, there are disadvantages: when you go back more than thirteen generations, the numbers get large and unwieldy. Another disadvantage is that you have to blot out and write new numbers for each ancestor on pedigree charts beyond the fifth generation.

The Doane-Bell System

We suggest you read the comments on numbering by Gilbert Doane and James Bell in their book, *Searching for Your Ancestors*; their system may be the best for you.

THE ANCESTOR CHART

This completed chart shows you how information may be entered on the ancestor charts. Enter a husband and wife together on an ancestor chart. If either marries more than once, you must fill out an ancestor chart for each marriage. Included in this kit are sixteen ancestor charts.

In addition to knowing your own line of descent from ancestor X, it is frequently useful as well as interesting to know the aunts and uncles and at least the brothers, sisters and first cousins of your ancestors. The ancestor chart is accordingly the most important single record you will keep.

ANCESTOR CHART				SURNAME STILES		

HUSBAND DANIEL STILES   THE SAME PERSON AS NO. 1   ON CHART 70
BORN April 11, 1787
WHERE
WHEN MARRIED   WHERE
DIED April 12, 1848
WHERE
HUSBAND'S FATHER Deacon AARON STILES CHART NO. 70   MOTHER CATHRINE CONKLIN CHART NO. 70
HUSBAND'S OTHER WIVES

WIFE Maiden Name SARAH BURROWS   THE SAME PERSON AS NO. 1   ON CHART 87
BORN Sept. 6, 1790
WHERE "In Vermont"
DIED July 9, 1864-5
WHERE
WIFE'S FATHER HUBBARD BURROWS III CHART NO. 87   MOTHER MARY WILKINS CHART NO. 87
WIFE'S OTHER HUSBANDS None

Child	Sex	CHILDREN of this marriage	BORN Date Place	DIED Date Place	MARRIED TO Date Place
1	F	Mary Stiles	May 26, 1806 Tompkins, N.Y.		Jonas Underwood Oct. 30, 1829 Tompkins, NY
2	F	Priscilla Stiles	Feb. 5, 1810 Tompkins, N.Y.	August 1874 Meadville, PA	Morris Coburn 1831, Tompkins, N.Y.
3	F	Lucy Stiles	Oct. 13, 1816 Tompkins, NY	Dec. 23, 1858 Humphrey, Cattaraugus, NY	Ezra Smith Oct. 28, 1844 Tompkins, NY
4	F	Sarah Stiles	April 3, 1819 Tompkins, N.Y.	July 17, 1877 Paterson, NJ	Rev. James Lloyd Breck Oct. 18, 1865 St. Louis, MA
5	F	Betsy Stiles	Nov. 29, 1822 Tompkins, NY		Parker Smith 1845
6	F	Leipha Stiles	Oct. 24, 1825 Tompkins, NY		John Meacham 1852
7	M	Charles Stiles	April 17, 1827 Tompkins, NY	Oct. 3, 1874 Delaware Co, NY	Thirza Beebe 1848
8	M	Edward Stiles	Sept. 9, 1829 Tompkins, N.Y.		Samantha Sackett 1861 Dunkirk, NY
9	F	Lavinia Stiles	Jan 7, 1831 Tompkins, NY		Henry Pierce 1852 Cattaraugus Co, NY
10					
11					
12					

SOURCES OF INFORMATION or documentation
The Stiles Family in America H.R. Stiles, Jersey City, 1895
Stilesville Cemetary, Stilesville, Delaware Co, N.Y. Visits 1924, 1941, 1973
Date 2-1-1977
Compiler P.S. Breck
Address 2140 Shattuck Ave.
Berkeley, CA 94704
City State Zip

Note:
Both Deacon Aaron Stiles and his father Stephen Stiles served in the American armed forces during the Revolution. So too did Hubbard Burrows III.

OTHER TYPES OF CHARTS

Another type of genealogical or pedigree chart is called a "pie chart." On page 7 is an example of such a chart, showing the ancestry of Hubbard Burrows III, who is ancestor #2 on Chart #87 on page 3. The example is greatly reduced from a wall chart of the sort you can make yourself or buy from many genealogical supply houses. There are other charts available with which you will become familiar as you progress.

The particular genealogy shown on the pie chart is unique in that there are published genealogies for every

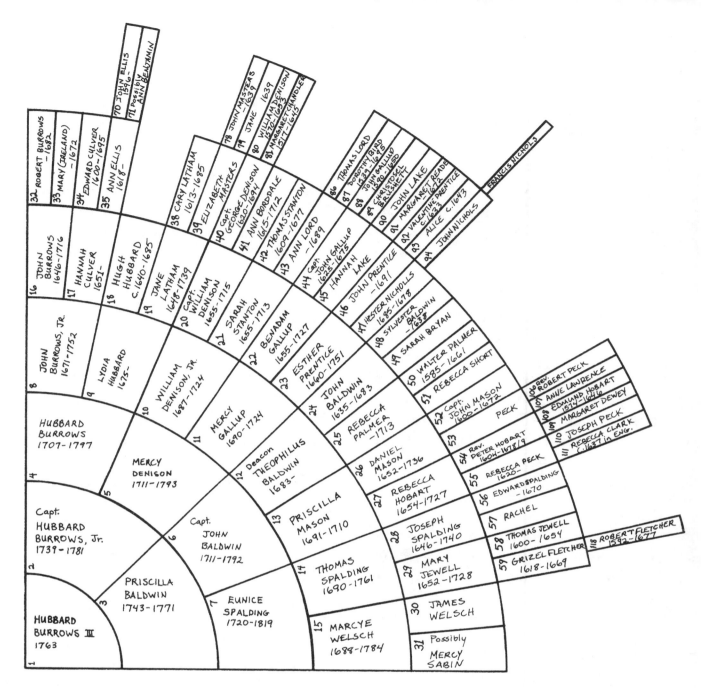

surname shown. Thus, while we have been unable to trace the ancestry of Hubbard Burrows III's wife, Mary Wilkins (87-3), we have been able to trace her husband's ancestry back to all of his immigrant ancestors.

CHERCHEZ LA FEMME

In ancestor hunting you should take the advice of that legendary detective who said, "Look for the woman." Always look for the female lines. Seek out any document that might have a woman's maiden name. Your most interesting ancestors are likely to be somewhere among your grandmother's people!

WORDS OF WARNING

There are hundreds of problems in ancestor hunting. Here are just a few about which you should be forewarned.

Evidence

Do not believe everything that is printed in a book. Many published family histories, and local histories, contain gross inaccuracies caused by sloppy research, wishful thinking, leaping to conclusions and even outright fabrications by people who were deliberately trying to graft famous names to the family tree by hook or by crook.

Once fabrications occur in published genealogies, the error is often copied and repeated over and over again in other books. As a general rule, genealogical "proof" should be based on at least two original records (court documents, letters and diaries, etc.) and you should be very dubious of authors who do not cite their sources.

Verbal Evidence

The law tends to regard eyewitness testimony as the best evidence, but also recognizes that memories can be faulty. The law also draws a clear distinction between eyewitness testimony about things a person actually saw and experienced, and "hearsay evidence."

A person who starts tracing his or her family roots by interviewing older relatives needs to keep these distinctions clearly in mind. Don't fall into the emotional trap of assuming that "Aunt Ida said it, so it must be true." Memories of old people, and even young ones, can be faulty when it comes to names, residences, dates of births, marriages and deaths, and other data.

Take good notes, and try to record interviews with older relatives by audio or video recorder. Ask questions to try to pin down specific facts about dates and places; then carefully evaluate each statement. Is it eyewitness evidence of something a person actually saw and experienced, or is it hearsay evidence which a person learned secondhand? Hearsay evidence can be extremely valuable and sometimes may be the best or only evidence available ---- but it should be accepted as factual only if it can be independently verified by contemporary documents.

Examples of hearsay evidence were the family traditions passed down by the descendants of Kunte Kinte. Neither Alex Haley nor his oldest surviving relatives were eyewitnesses to most of the events which Haley described in his bestselling book, *Roots*. Haley's research involved tracking down contemporary documents of things that happened to his ancestors hundreds of years ago.

Each statement of verbal evidence should be evaluated carefully. Is it eyewitness or hearsay? For example, an elderly woman who was the youngest child in a large family may be wrong about the order of birth of her older brothers and sisters. Her recollections about this are hearsay. The eldest daughter in a large family, however, probably had to help care for her siblings and can provide eyewitness recollections on birth order; she probably has an accurate memory of the birth date, or at least the birth year, for each sibling.

Sometimes even people very close to others are misinformed. One of our great-grandmothers was insistent that she was descended from a Colonel Thomas Terry who gained some distinction in the American Revolution. She insisted her grandmother, whom she knew and dearly loved, was Colonel Terry's daughter. Unfortunately it turned out that Colonel Terry's daughter was her grandfather's *second* wife; his first wife was her real grandmother.

The same great-grandmother carefully recorded the name of her great-great-grandmother Wells as Jemima Skillman. Skillman turned out to be Jemima's second husband's name while her maiden name was Overton. This resulted in considerable confusion and a great deal of time spent in tracing Skillman rather than Overton ancestors.

Stories told to you by parents and grandparents about things that happened to them before you were born (or before you were old enough to be an eyewitness) are obviously hearsay evidence, although you probably have accepted such statements without question. Errors in transmission creep in when your grandparents relate stories they heard from their grandparents. Try to verify this kind of hearsay evidence with contemporary documents.

There are times, however, when hearsay evidence is superior to court records. A person disinherits a son or a daughter, or a child dies before his parents. The child's name does not appear in the parents' will, so the hearsay account of the person's existence is very important.

Similarly, you may have an ancestral family with six children, although only five births appear in the church register. Through hearsay evidence, you learn that the parents were living temporarily in another town (whose church register had been destroyed) when the sixth child was born. You have a duty to posterity to record that piece of information, stating who told it to you and from whom they heard it.

SEARCHING RECORDS

Genealogy, like history, is constructed on a foundation of written records. Almost any surviving record may be valuable to a genealogist. To some extent this distorts the search for our roots, because the types of records our society commonly preserves have tended to filter out women, urban craftsmen living in rented homes and a host of other people.

The primary records our society preserves are:

1. **Birth Records**. Birth certificates (during the past century or so) usually have been filed in the county courthouse and also in the state capitol. They list parents' names as well as dates of birth.

2. **Death Records**. Death certificates are also usually on file in county courthouses and usually list parents' names and places of birth.

3. **Land Records**. In most states, every time real estate changes hands, title searchers go back and re-record the names of all previous owners. Original records may vanish, but these copies survive.

4. **Military Records**. Victorious armies are commemorated with statues, medals, booty and song. Retreating armies are usually too busy to keep good records, but military records remain a great source of ancestor information.

5. **Public Office**. Our society tends to preserve the names of elected and appointed public officials, but not always. A "lost mayor" of San Francisco recently was found by historians and there are "lost governors" of Colonial Pennsylvania.

6. **Criminal Records**. Criminal records, or more precisely *criminal justice system records*, have been key documents in tracing many of America's leading families, although some professional genealogists have used considerable artistry to disguise their source of information.

7. **Court Cases**. Divorces, contested wills, quit title actions, slander suits, paternity suits and similar cases can be a gold mine for a genealogical researcher, because they cause patterns of family relationships to be spread out on the public record.

8. **Church Records**. Until modern times in the United States and Europe, it was the churches, not the state, which kept vital records such as births (baptisms), marriages and deaths. In Sweden this is still true.

9. **Census Records**. Microfilm copies of complete original census sheets from the year 1790 to 1910 are available in many large public libraries, Family History Centers of the Church of Latter-Day Saints and regional offices of the National Archives. Some early censuses are indexed and published in book form, and some commercial services provide computer printouts of all similar names on the census record.

10. **Cemeteries**. Tombstones and their relationship to other tombstones and grave registers can provide much valuable data.

11. **Newspaper Files**. Most people make their hometown newspapers when they are born, graduated, married, divorced, arrested, robbed, win trophies, enlist in or are separated from the armed forces, and die. If you know the date and area one of your ancestors did one of these things, check the newspapers in the area for a report. Obituaries are particularly good sources.

12. **Wills**. Wills are the mainstay of genealogy and provide much data found nowhere else. Wills and probate administrative records (showing how assets were distributed) are usually public records on file in the nation's more than 3,000 county courthouses.

13. **Life Insurance Policies, Old Correspondence, Diaries, Family Books and Photograph Albums**.

14. **Account Books** and other records of financial transactions.

15. **Any Record** that can supply you with information about your ancestors.

COLLATERAL RELATIONSHIPS

Part of the fun of genealogy is finding out about some of your interesting, and perhaps important, distant cousins. If their ancestry is the subject of a book or article, it makes it easier to trace your own ancestry.

Presidential Connections

Cornelius A. Garretson (whom his dad said will be President in 2012) is the son of a former Oakland newspaperman, "Skip" Garretson, a fourteenth generation American whose ancestors came to Plymouth on the Mayflower in 1620. His mother, Maureen, is the daughter of Cornelius Mulholland, a veteran of the Irish War for Independence who came to America 300 years later in the 1920s.

The chart on page 12 shows young Cornelius to be a distant cousin of four American presidents of various degrees of reputation, of the notorious Revolutionary firebrand Sam Adams, and of the great orator Daniel Webster. The chart on page 5 sets forth the American ancestry of former British Prime Minister Winston Churchill, to whom young Cornelius is also distantly related (did you know, by the way, that Winnie was part American Indian?).

Parallel Lines of Descent

All of us are descended from both kings and slaves, and the excitement of modern ancestor hunting is not finding a status-giving ancestor, it is knowing all of the people whose lives and loves influenced ours.

Most people who trace even one leg of their ancestry back to colonial America are probably related to at least one president of the United States. It is not uncommon for people to find they are related to a dozen presidents.

As you delve into your own ancestry, you will observe astonishing interrelationships and probably discover some unsuspected famous (and perhaps infamous) branches in your family tree.

The chart on the following page shows just a few alliances of future President Cornelius A. Garretson, stemming from only two of his known ancestors twelve generations ago.

Simple population mathematics shows that in the twelfth generation back, each of us could have 2,048 ancestors (the number is usually reduced by marriages of cousins with common ancestors). Each ancestor by now probably has tens of thousands ---- perhaps millions ---- of descendants. A politician who could trace all of his living cousins, and get them to vote for him, probably could win just about any election!

SOURCES OF INFORMATION

Many records can be found only in the offices of county and city clerks, the church to which an ancestor belonged, or in the archives in a state or the nation's capitol.

There are genealogical libraries in most large cities and many smaller ones. Many genealogical and historical societies have excellent libraries. (Check the yellow pages of your local telephone book for their addresses and phone numbers.) Your local librarian can be of tremendous help to you in putting you in touch with various organizations, and many books can be procured through your local library on interbranch loan.

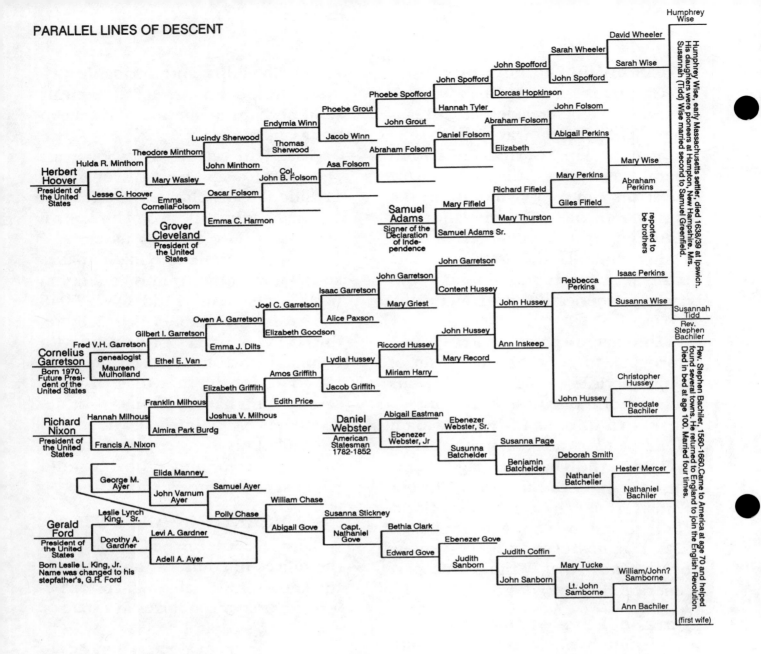

Published Genealogies

Published genealogies of families with the same surname as yours (not only your father's name, but all the names borne by your ancestors) are frequently available. Many of these books will be in a genealogical library near you. There are published bibliographies of genealogies in the Library of Congress and in other libraries.

Genealogically Concerned Societies

Patriotic, ethnic, religious, historical, heraldic and hereditary societies can provide useful genealogical information.

State and local historical societies have important files or genealogical material such as letters, diaries, old business records, and obscure and local books and periodicals. Many amateurs who start out as genealogy buffs become proficient historians as they try to learn more about the life and times of their ancestors.

The DAR (Daughters of the American Revolution) and the SAR (Sons of the American Revolution) are particularly famous for their genealogical records, but similar records are sometimes maintained by ethnic societies of Polish, Irish, Czech, German, Italian, Greek and other ancestral heritage organizations.

You can often find portions of your ancestry already researched for you by some distant relative in the files of hereditary societies which require members to submit family trees tracing back to a Mayflower passenger, a European king, a Confederate soldier, a colonial American property owner, or whatever.

Not to be overlooked are the scores of family associations who seek to maintain records of everyone bearing a particular surname or descended from someone with such surname.

Church records, particularly for smaller sects such as Quakers and Mennonites, are extremely valuable. H.H. Hinshaw has published a six-volume digest of references of genealogical importance in older American Quaker records.

The Garretson Society, which published a national genealogical newspaper for decades, consisted of the thousands of descendants of one sailor on a Dutch ship which ran aground on Long Island in 1657 while delivering supplies to the Dutch Colony in Delaware.

Many people are interested in heraldry, the study of "armorial insignia," or coats-of-arms. Some people claim coats-of-arms representing each surname in their family tree, although experts say that technically, simply having the same name is not enough. A coat-of-arms really belongs only to the actual descendants of the man first authorized to emblazon his shield with his personal armorial insignia.

Many coats-of-arms now circulated in the United States are fabrications, mass-produced by gnomes in the cyclone cellars of Ohio and the art sweat shops of Manhattan. Good genealogists will not claim a coat-of-arms unless they can establish an authentic line.

FAMILY RECORDS AND PHOTOGRAPHS

The family records and photographs you have or will collect form a unique genealogical and historical resource. With a little imagination, many of the original records (or copies of them) can be framed or mounted for display as priceless family heirlooms.

By making good, inexpensive photo copies of government documents, such as military commissions, land title patents and invention patent papers (all of which used to be signed by the President of the United States), you can both preserve valuable genealogical records and create heirlooms that are interesting conversation pieces for the walls of your home.

Copies of wills, court oaths, immigration papers, pages from ship records, election, census and estate administration documents, as well as copies of old survey maps listing ancestral property by the owner's name, are not only documents for inclusion in your family history but also for framing. For example, using the county's precise legal description of land sold to an ancestor by the government, we obtained from the U.S. Department of the Interior, a 22-x-10½-inch reproduction of a land patent issued to Rev. Joel C. Garretson, signed by President John Tyler in 1841.

Using copy negatives and a little imagination, you can create very unusual displays. For example, photographs of five generations of Garretsons as young men are displayed in a 22½-x- 6¼-inch wall frame (here, an artist's rendition). Joel and Owen were enlarged from full-length photos on tiny, scratched tintypes where their faces were only millimeters wide. Gilbert was enlarged from a college class photo in which he was one of 156 faces in a crowd. The captions are typed onto standard gummed labels.

THE NATIONAL ARCHIVES

The National Archives is probably the single most important source of data for American genealogists. However, to use these records effectively, you have to have a very specific idea of what you're looking for.

For the genealogical researcher, the National Archives may be a golden treasure trove, or an endless swamp. In order to find your way, every beginning genealogist should

Rev. Joel C. Garretson 1809-1895
son of Isaac Garretson 1765-1844

Owen A. Garretson 1852-1933

Gilbert I. Garretson 1899-1941

Fred V. H. Garretson, b. 1934

Cornelius A. Garretson, b. 1970

write to:

National Archives Records Service
Washington, DC 20408

and ask for these free forms and publications:

- *Genealogical Records in the National Archives*, Leaflet No. 5. It tells you how to find old naturalization records, immigration passenger lists, passport applications, lists of passengers going through customs, certain land records, some government records relating to Indians who retained their tribal status, federal personnel records prior to 1910, census records and other data.

Some records aren't available unless they're more than 75 years old, but there are procedures through which some more recent records can be obtained. A more detailed publication, *Guide to Genealogical Records in the National Archives* (GS 4.6/2: G28), a 1964 publication, is available in hard cover or paperback from the U.S. Government Printing Office, Washington, DC 20402.

- *GSA Form 80*, which is needed to apply for copies of military service, pension and land-bounty records. Photocopies of records of United States (or Confederate) soldiers, sailors and marines who served more than 75 years ago are available for reasonable fees (GSA sends the bill to you along with the documents). Pension applications are particularly valuable because the applicant usually had to put down a lot of information about himself and his military and civilian careers. Indexes of these military records are available in branch offices of the Archives. Photocopies of records can be ordered directly by sending Form 80 to: General Reference Branch, National Archives and Administration (NNRGP), 7 Pennsylvania Ave. NW, Washington, DC 20408.

The National Archives, headquartered in Washington, DC has eleven branch offices around the nation which store original records from federal agencies having their regional headquarters in nearby cities. However, records involving the same town may be scattered in several different branches of the Archives because different federal agencies have (or had) different boundaries and sent records to different depositories. The branches hold about one-third of all the National Archives' records, receiving 750,000 cubic feet of records a year and destroying 600,000 cubic feet annually.

In addition to regional office records, the branch offices also have microfilm copies of many records kept in Washington.

Some branches have concentrations of records of special genealogical interest to some ethnic groups. New York has records of Puerto Ricans; San Francisco has a major collection of Samoan records plus many records dealing with people of Chinese and Japanese ancestry. Fort Worth has many records concerning Mexican-Americans.

Branch Offices of the National Archives

Boston: 380 Trapelo Road, Waltham, MA 02154, (617)647-8100. Stores federal records from Connecticut, Maine, Massachusetts, New Hampshire, Rhode Island and Vermont.

New Jersey: Building 22-MOT, Bayonne, NJ 07002, (201)823-7252. Serves New Jersey, New York, Puerto Rico and the Virgin Islands.

Philadelphia: 9th and Market Sts., Room 1350, Philadelphia, PA 19107, (215)597-3000. Serves Delaware and Pennsylvania and also stores microfilm records for the District of Columbia, Maryland, Virginia and West Virginia.

Atlanta: 1557 St. Joseph Ave., East Point, GA 30344, (404)763-7477. Serves Alabama, Georgia, Florida, Kentucky, Mississippi, North Carolina, South Carolina and Tennessee.

Chicago: 7358 South Pulaski Road, Chicago, IL 60629, (312)581-7816. Serves Illinois, Indiana, Michigan, Minnesota, Ohio and Wisconsin. (There is a branch of the Chicago Archives in Dayton, Ohio.)

Kansas City: 2312 East Bannister Road, Kansas City, MO 64131, (816)926-6272. Serves Iowa, Kansas, Missouri and Nebraska.

Fort Worth: 501 West Felix Street, P.O. Box 6216, Fort Worth, TX 76115, (817)334-5525. Serves Arkansas, Louisiana, New Mexico, Oklahoma and Texas.

Denver: Building 48, Denver Federal Center, Denver, CO 80225, (303)236-0817. Serves Colorado, Montana, North Dakota, Utah and Wyoming.

San Francisco: 1000 Commodore Drive, San Bruno, CA 94066, (415)876-9009. Serves Northern California, Hawaii, Nevada (except Clark County), and the Pacific Ocean territories including American Samoa.

Los Angeles: 24000 Avila Road, Laguna Niguel, CA 92677, (714)643-4241. Serves all of Arizona; Clark County, Nevada; and eleven Southern California counties.

Seattle: 6125 Sand Point Way NE, Seattle, WA 98115, (206)526-6507. Serves Alaska, Idaho, Oregon and Washington.

GENEALOGICAL LIBRARIES

To list all of the genealogical libraries in the United States would make this beginner's kit cumbersome, but in the following pages we list some of the more important of them. The examples we have given are based primarily upon the size of the collections and this does not mean that these are the *best* libraries in all ways. Many smaller libraries, even very small specialized libraries, often contain rare books and unpublished manuscripts not available anywhere else.

A comprehensive listing of genealogical resources is available in *The Genealogist's Address Book* by Elizabeth Petty Bentley, Genealogical Publishing Co., Baltimore, MD.

A very extensive, state-by-state list of genealogical libraries, genealogical societies, genealogical periodicals and professional genealogists (listing their spheres of speciation) is published annually in *The Genealogical Helper,* an important ancestor research magazine available in most libraries with genealogical collections. It is published by Everton Publishing Co., 526 North Main Street, Logan, UT 84321.

The Library of Congress

A must-stop in Washington, DC for any genealogist is the Library of Congress, Genealogical Department, Library of Congress Annex, Washington, DC 20540. Extensive genealogical resources, including the Charles Edward Banks Collection.

Family History Centers, Church of Jesus Christ of Latter-Day Saints

A comprehensive list of these libraries can be found in *The Library, A Guide to the LDS Family History Library*, from Ancestry, Inc.

There are more than 1,400 Family History Centers, found at many Mormon Temples throughout the United States and the world. In addition to books and microfilm of raw data such as parish registers, these Family History Centers contain photostats of family bibles and files of ancestry records compiled by Mormon Church members whose religious duty requires them to do genealogical research in order to discover and baptize their ancestors. Family History Centers can be found in the following cities in the United States:

Alabama: Huntsville; **Arizona**: Flagstaff, Glove, Holbrook, Mesa, Phoenix (3), Prescott, Safford, St. David, St. Johns, Show Low, Snowflake, Tucson, Yuma; **Arkansas**: Little Rock; **California**: Anaheim, Bakersfield, Barstow, Cerritos, Chico, Covina, Escondido, Eureka, Fresno, Gridley, La Crescenta, Lancaster, Lompoc, Long Beach, Los Angeles (2), Menlo Park, Modesto, Mission Viejo, Norwalk, Oakland, Sacramento, San Bernardino, San Diego, San Jose, San Luis Obispo, Santa Barbara, Santa Clara, Santa Rosa, Seaside, Simi Valley, Stockton, Upland, Ventura;

Colorado: Arvada, Boulder, Colorado Springs, Denver, Northglenn, Cortez, Fort Collins, Grand Junction, LaJara, Littleton, Glenwood Springs; **Connecticut**: Manchester; **Florida**: Jacksonville, Orange Park, Miami, Orlando, Pensacola, Tallahassee, Tampa; **Georgia**: Macon, Dunwoody; **Hawaii**: Honolulu, Kaneohe, Laie; **Idaho**: Blackfoot, Boise, Burley, Driggs, Idaho Falls, Lewiston, Malad, Montpelier, Moore, Pocatelo, Texburg, Salmon, Twin Falls;

Illinois: Champaign, Chicago Heights, Naperville, Wilmett; **Indiana**: Fort Wayne, Indianapolis; **Iowa**: West Des Moines; **Kansas**: Manhattan, Wichita; **Kentucky**: Lexington, Louisville; **Louisiana**: Baton Rouge; **Maine**: Farmingdale; **Maryland**: Silver Spring; **Massachusetts**: Weston; **Michigan**: Bloomfield Hills, Dearborn, Lansing, Midland; **Minnesota**: Minneapolis; **Mississippi**: Hattiesburg; **Missouri**: Kansas City, Frontenac, South Columbia, Springfield; **Montana**: Billings, Dillon, Great Falls, Helena, Kalispell, Missoula;

Nebraska: Omaha; **Nevada**: Elko, Ely, Fallon, Las Vegas, Reno; **New Hampshire**: Manchester; **New Jersey**: East Brunswick, Summit; **New Mexico**: Albuquerque, Farmington, Las Cruces, Roswell; **New York**: Albany, Buffalo, Fairport, New York City, Plainview, Vistal; **North Carolina**: Charlotte, Kinston, Raleigh, Wilmington; **Ohio**: Cincinatti, Westlake, Reynoldsburg, Dayton;

Oklahoma: Oklahoma City, Tulsa; **Oregon**: Beaverton, Bend, North Bend, Corvallis, Eugene, Gresham, Klamath Falls, LaGrande, Medford, The Dalles, Nyssa, Oregon City, Portland, Myrtle Creek, Salem; **Pennsylvania**: York, Broomall, State College; **South Carolina**: Columbia; **Tennessee**: Knoxville, Memphis, Madison, Tullahoma;

Texas: Austin, Corpus Christi, Dallas, El Paso, Fort Worth, Houston, Longview, Odessa, San Antonio, Vidor; **Utah**: Beaver, Brigham City, Logan, Cedar City, Delta, Duchesne, Filmore, Heber City, North Blanding, Mt. Pleasant, Ogden, Price, Richfield, Roosevelt, Salt Lake City, Santaquin, South Jordan, St. George, Springville, Vernal, Provo;

Virginia: Annandale, Virginia Beach, Oakton, Richmond; **Washington**: Bellevue, Bremerton, Everett, Longview, Moses Lake, Mt. Vernon, Olympia, Pasco, Sumner, Quincy, Richland, Seattle, Spokane, Tacoma, Vancouver, Yakima; **Wisconsin**: Shawano, Hales Corner; **Wyoming**: Afton, Casper, Cheyenne, Cody, Evanston, Lovell, Rock Springs.

GENEALOGICAL SOCIETY LIBRARIES

There are more than 400 genealogical societies or genealogical sections of historical societies in the United States; many have excellent genealogical collections. Among the more noted are:

New England Historic Genealogical Society, 101 Newbury Street, Boston, MA 02116, (617)536-5740. The oldest, large genealogical library in the United States has many unpublished manuscripts and puts out the New England Historical and Genealogical Register. The society has a nation-wide membership.

The National Genealogical Society, 4527 -17th St. North, Arlington, VA 22207, (703)525-0050.

New York Genealogical and Biographical Society Library, 122-126 East 58th Street, New York, NY 10022, (212)755-8532. Publishes a major genealogical journal and has church records, cemetery inscriptions, abstracts of wills, bible records, etc.

The Genealogical Society of Pennsylvania, 1300 Locust St., Philadelphia, PA 19107, (215)545-0391.

PUBLIC LIBRARIES

Some of the finest genealogical libraries are public, such as:

New York Public Library, American History and Genealogical Division, Fifth Avenue and 42nd Street, New York, NY 10017 (P.O. Box 2237, Grand Central Station, New York, NY 10017), (212)930-0828. One of the largest in the country, with important resources on European lineages.

Connecticut State Library, 231 Capitol Avenue, Hartford, CT 06115, (203)566-3692. One of the best collections in the country.

Pennsylvania State Library, Genealogy Section, Walnut and Commonwealth Avenue, Education Building (P.O. Box 1601) Harrisburg, PA 17105, (717)783-5991.

Public Library of Fort Wayne and Allen County, 900 Webster St., P.O. Box 2270, Fort Wayne, IN 46802, (219)424-7241, Ext. 2242.

St. Louis Public Library, 1301 Olive Street, St. Louis, MO 63103.

California State Library, Sutro Branch, 480 Winston Dr., San Francisco, CA 94132, (415)731-4477. This library specializes in an outstanding collection of local history and genealogy of the other 49 states and Europe. The California Section of the state library is located at 914 Capitol Mall, P.O. Box 942837, Sacramento, CA 94237, (916)445-4149.

Los Angeles Public Library, History Department and Genealogy Room, 630 West Fifth Street, Los Angeles, CA 90071, (213)612-3317. An excellent and growing collection.

Grand Rapids Public Library, 60 Library Plaza NE, Grand Rapids, MI 49503, (616)456-3640.

Detroit Public Library, 5201 Woodward Avenue, Detroit, MI 48202, (313)833-1480. Houses the Burton Historical Collection and issues the Detroit Society for Genealogical Research Magazine.

Public Library of Cincinnati and Hamilton County, Library Square, 800 Vine St., Cincinnati, OH 45202, (513)369-6900.

Cleveland Public Library, 325 Superior Avenue, Cleveland, OH 44114, (216)623-2864.

Dallas Public Library, Genealogy Section, 1515 Young St., Dallas, TX 75201, (214)670-1433.

Chattanooga-Hamilton County Public Library, Genealogy Dept., 1001 Broad St., Chattanooga, TN 37402, (615)757-5317.

Joint Free Public Library of Morristown and Morris Township, 1 Miller Rd., P.O. Box 267M, Morristown, NJ 07960, (201)538-3473.

There is a public library in almost every American city, town and hamlet and a state library in every state. The quality and size of their genealogical collections and the genealogical competence of their staffs varies, but it is a mistake not to investigate their resources, particularly in towns in which your ancestors lived. At worst, the librarian in your town can probably steer you to the best sources of genealogical information in your area.

HISTORICAL SOCIETIES

Many historical societies have excellent genealogical collections. Among the best are:

Rhode Island State Historical Society, 121 Hope St., Providence, RI 02909, (401)331-8575.

State Historical Society of Wisconsin, 816 State Street, Madison, WI 53706, (608)262-9590.

Bucks County Historical Society, P.O. Box 1092, Doylestown, PA 18901.

Minnesota Historical Society, 690 Cedar Street, St. Paul, MN 55101,

(612)296-2143.

Brooklyn Historical Society, 128 Pierpont Street, Brooklyn, NY 11201,(718)624-0890.

New York Historical Society, 170 Central Park West, New York City, NY 10024, (212)873-3400. Emphasizes New York and northeastern states.

New London County Historical Society, 11 Blinman Street, New London, CT 06320, (203)443-1209.

Massachusetts Historical Society, 1154 Boylston St., Boston, MA 02215, (617)536-1608.

Maryland Historical Society, 201 West Monument Street, Baltimore, MD 21201, (301)685-3750, Ext. 359.

There are many more. Some of the better local collections are housed in local historical society libraries. One of the excellent collections we have browsed in is that of the Suffolk County Historical Society in Riverhead, Long Island, New York. Such local societies as the Stonington Historical Society in Stonington, Connecticut, are primary sources of genealogical information in their area.

HEREDITARY SOCIETIES

There are many organizations in the United States in which membership is restricted to descendants of particular categories of ancestors; each has archives containing much valuable genealogical information. The most noted of these libraries is:

Daughters of the American Revolution Memorial Library, 1776 D Street NW, Washington, DC 20006, (202)879-3229. This large library is open to the public except during the DAR Continental Congress in the spring. In addition to books and documents, the DAR library has available half a million membership applications showing valuable information about descendants of Revolutionary War Patriots. The lineage books published by the society are in many American libraries.

PRIVATE COLLECTIONS

There are many great private genealogical collections in various parts of the country. Among the more noted are:

Godfrey Memorial Library, 134 Newfield Street, Middletown, CT 06475, (203)346-4375. In addition to a large library, it has a file of more than seven million genealogical references and has microcard publications.

Newberry Library, 60 West Walton Street, Chicago, IL 60610, (312)943-9090.

Huntington Library, San Marino, CA 91108, (818)405-2141.

UNIVERSITY LIBRARIES

The great historical collections at our major universities and many of our smaller colleges contain rich veins of genealogical material, but the rules for their use frequently restrict genealogical research by non-academic researchers. You should make inquiry regarding each library's rules before seeking to do research in their collections.

BOOKS ON GENEALOGY

There are many good books on genealogy. A few are especially recommended:

Searching for Your Ancestors, Gilbert H. Doane and James B. Bell, University of Minnesota Press, Minneapolis, MN 55114, 1980, revised 1993.

Handy Book for Genealogists, Everton Publishers.

The Genealogist's Address Book, Elizabeth Petty Bentley, Genealogical Publishing Co., Baltimore, MD.

Building an American Pedigree, Norman Wright, Brigham Young University, Provo, UT.

The Researcher's Guide to American Genealogy, Val. D. Greenwood, Genealogical Publishing Co., Baltimore, MD, 1975.

The Source, Eakle and Cerny, Ancestry, Inc. (Guidebook of American Genealogy).

Among helpful books and manuals regarding genealogical research in the British Isles are these:

English Genealogy, Sir Anthony Wagner, Oxford, 1960.

Tracing Your Ancestors, Anthony J. Camp, John Gifford Ltd., London, 1964.

Introducing Family History, Cecil R. Humphrey-Smith, Family History, Northgate, Canterbury, 1975.

A Handbook on Irish Genealogy, Wallace Clare (1937, revised 1966), The Irish Genealogical Research Society, London, 1975.

Genealogists' Handbook, Peter Spufford and Anthony J. Camp, issued by the Society of Genealogists, London, 1969.

Some other good specialized books are:

Finding Our Fathers. A Guide-book to Jewish Genealogy, Dan Rottenberg, Random House, New York, 1977.

Chinese Studies in Federal Records, Jo Ann Williamson, issued by National Archives and Record Service, U.S. General Services Administration, San Bruno, CA; U.S. Government Printing Office: 1975-694-277/128.

The Atlantic Bridge to Germany, Charles M. Hall, two volumes, The Everton Publishers, Logan, UT, 1974.

Encyclopedia of German-American Genealogical Research, Clifford Neal and Anna P.C. Smith, R.R. Bowker Co., New York, 1976.

Dictionnaire Genealogique des Familles Canadiennes, Quebec 1871-1890. Seven volumes, some reprinted by the Genealogical Publishing Co., Baltimore, MD.

PUBLISHING A FAMILY HISTORY

After you have visited several libraries and inspected a number of very elaborate published genealogies (some can be thousands of pages in length and many volumes; others are bound in leather and contain costly colored engravings and charts), you may think a published family history is out of the range of your pocketbook. Don't. One hundred copies of a brief 24-page family history with photographs and copy as shown on page 23 and charts similar to those used in this manual can cost you as little as several hundred dollars (if you personally type the copy and paste up your "layout" for the printer; or better yet, if you use a computer and a desktop publishing package).

A good format involves listing all the known ancestors and descendants of a specific ancestor, or ancestral couple. You'll need charts, of course, but mainly you'll want to record narrative material: anecdotes about aunts, ancestors and cousins, the environment in which they lived, the location of their homes (and what stands there now), the "who, what, where, when, why and how" of their lives, and a bit of the history of their towns and the events in which they participated and which they witnessed.

Photos and other illustrations are not necessary in a family history, but they make it much more interesting.

In the example on the facing page, the caption merely places in narrative form the information given for ancestors 14 and 15 on Chart #1, page 3; adding for the sake of interest quotes from Charles and Mary Kirkpatrick's diaries.

Copyright the published book (two copies will then be in the Library of Congress) and donate copies to your local public and genealogical libraries. Future researchers and your descendants will bless you!

COMPUTERIZED GENEALOGY

With the advent and widespread use of personal computers, it was inevitable that genealogical research make use of this new technology.

There is no question that for a skilled genealogist who is also a skilled computer operator, computerization of genealogical research is highly desirable; but for a novice genealogist who is also a novice computer operator, it is doubtful that computerization is a wise course of action.

There are now on the market 50 or more genealogical computer programs ranging in price from $35 to $300. The "bestsellers" appear to be the LDS Church's *PAF (Personal Ancestral File), Roots III* and *Quansoft.* A computer program is the necessary means for causing a computer to function and all programs are not operational on all computers. The *PAF,* for example, runs on IBM, Apple II and Macintosh.

A good book on the subject is *Computer Genealogy,* by Richard A. Pence, Ancestry Inc., P.O. Box 476, Salt Lake City, UT 84110. Your local genealogical library or bookstore can advise you of other publications and articles.

Before you decide whether a computerized genealogy program is for you, proceed with your research as indicated in this book. The information you develop can be computerized later (if desirable), so no time will be lost.

Ancestry, Inc., publishes an excellent quarterly journal, *Genealogical Computers,* which contains articles regarding various developments and problems pertinent to the field.

Before deciding to computerize your research, make sure that you have or can develop the skills required to use a computer, and that the program you decide to use will work on the computer you have, or plan to acquire.

DR. CHARLES ALEXANDER KIRKPATRICK (1823-1892) AND MARY ANN (BENJAMIN) KIRKPATRICK (1834-1925)

A 49er, a physician, and a major in the Union Army during the Civil War, he was born in a cabin on the Mississippi on July 23, 1823. His earliest recollections were of an old double log cabin "with its great generous fireplace" and "cold winter nights when the event of the day was the return of Father from the hunt when he would roll in the back log and build a great crackling fire and we would gather around the hearth and listen with eager interest to his recital of the events of the day. . . " He died in San Francisco in April 1892.

A talented writer and the mother of nine children, she was born in Riverhead, Long Island on October 24, 1834. Her first memories were of head-high fields of red clover, Sunday dinners with her grandfather after he got through preaching at the Baiting Hollow church and her first school days at the young ladies' seminary in Riverhead. She came across the Isthmus of Panama in 1856 and married Dr. Kirkpatrick on September 29, aboard the ship that had brought her to California. She died in San Francisco on December 8, 1925.

FORMS

The two basic forms you will require as a dilettante genealogist are those contained in this book. As you progress to the search of census records, military records, legal records, immigration and naturalization records, etc., you may find you want other forms.

Most major genealogical societies and Family History Centers, many local societies and all genealogical supply houses offer forms for sale.

Two leading companies in the genealogical field are:

Ancestry, Inc., P.O. Box 476, Salt Lake City, UT 84110, 1-(800)531-1790.

Everton Publishers, Inc., P.O. Box 368, Logan, UT 84321, 1-(800)443-6325.

Both companies publish forms and on request will provide free catalogues of their many publications and services. Ancestry, Inc., publishes *Ancestry Magazine*, and Everton, *Genealogical Helper,* both bi-monthly publications containing valuable material on genealogy.

An excellent publication containing forms and designed as a permanent genealogical record is *Family History Record Book,* by James B. Bell, University of Minnesota Press, 2037 University Avenue Southeast, Minneapolis, MN 55414.

Advertisements in genealogical journals list many other sources, or you may wish to make up your own forms and have them printed by a small printer in your area.

There are no uniform forms for making up a "family tree" for wall display. There are many colorful forms available, but as no two genealogies are alike it is probable that you will have to devise your own with the help of a local artist or calligrapher. In the course of your research, you will see many charts which may appeal to you and you will probably want to pick and choose elements of several to prepare your own display family tree if you decide you want one.

This book is designed to give you only the fundamentals of genealogical research. There are a great many books, publications and courses of instruction that can provide you with specific techniques for advanced genealogical research.

You will probably also want to join one or more genealogical societies which offer continuing instruction on research in different geographic or ethnic areas as well as valuable contacts with other genealogists.

GENEALOGICAL CHART

CHART NO. _____

Date _____

Compiler _____

Address _____

_____

City   State   Zip

NO. 1 IS THE SAME PERSON AS NO. _____ ON CHART NO. _____

NAME
CONTINUED
ON CHART

FATHER

2
BORN
WHERE
WHEN MARRIED
DIED
WHERE

4
BORN
WHERE
WHEN MARRIED
DIED
WHERE

8
BORN
WHERE
WHEN MARRIED
DIED
WHERE

16

17

9
BORN
WHERE
DIED
WHERE

18

19

5
BORN
WHERE
DIED
WHERE

10
BORN
WHERE
WHEN MARRIED
DIED
WHERE

20

21

11
BORN
WHERE
DIED
WHERE

22

23

1
BORN
WHERE
WHEN MARRIED
DIED
WHERE

NAME OF HUSBAND OR WIFE

CHART NO._____

MOTHER

3
BORN
WHERE
DIED
WHERE

6
BORN
WHERE
WHEN MARRIED
DIED
WHERE

12
BORN
WHERE
WHEN MARRIED
DIED
WHERE

24

25

13
BORN
WHERE
DIED
WHERE

26

27

7
BORN
WHERE
DIED
WHERE

14
BORN
WHERE
WHEN MARRIED
DIED
WHERE

28

29

15
BORN
WHERE
DIED
WHERE

30

31

SOURCES OF INFORMATION

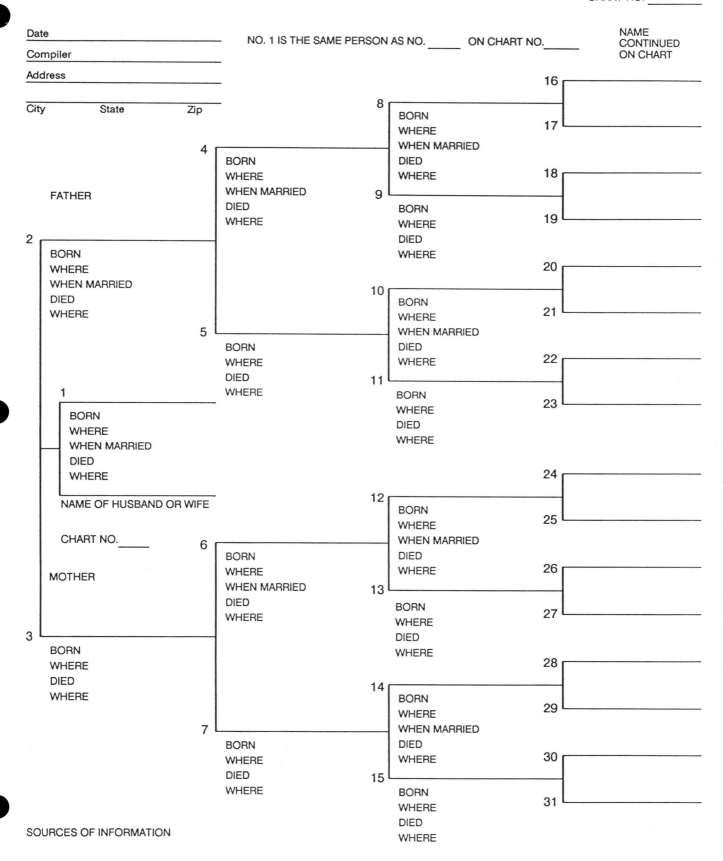

GENEALOGICAL CHART

CHART NO. ①

Date JUNE 17 1995

Compiler CHRIS BROWNE

Address 531 REID ST.

SARASOTA FL. 34242

City   State   Zip

NO. 1 IS THE SAME PERSON AS NO. _____ ON CHART NO. _____

NAME
CONTINUED
ON CHART

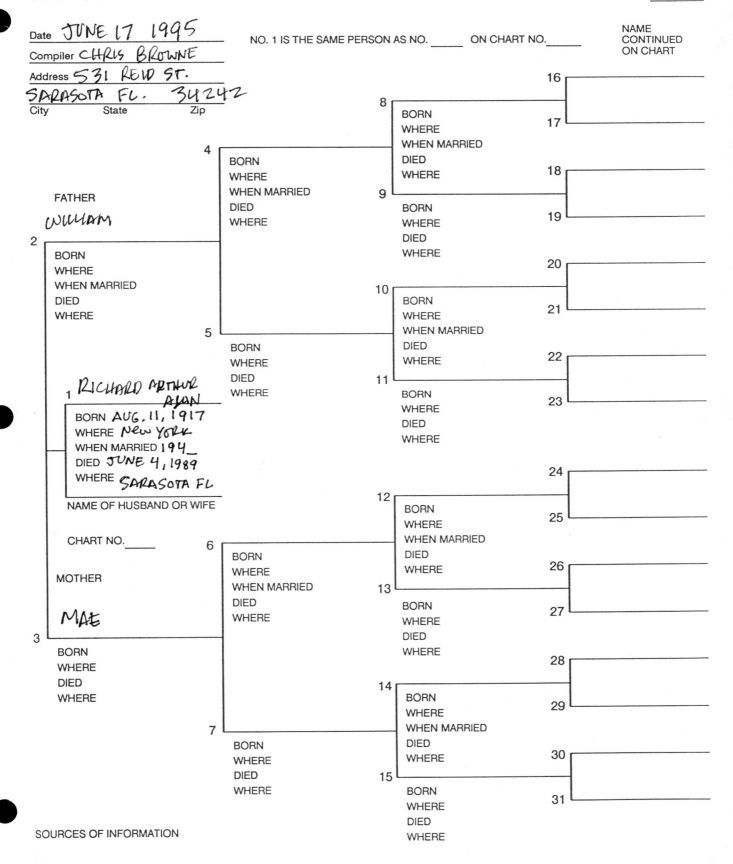

FATHER

WILLIAM

2
BORN
WHERE
WHEN MARRIED
DIED
WHERE

1 RICHARD ARTHUR
             ALAN
BORN AUG. 11, 1917
WHERE NEW YORK
WHEN MARRIED 194_
DIED JUNE 4, 1989
WHERE SARASOTA FL

NAME OF HUSBAND OR WIFE

CHART NO. _____

MOTHER

MAE

3
BORN
WHERE
DIED
WHERE

4
BORN
WHERE
WHEN MARRIED
DIED
WHERE

5
BORN
WHERE
DIED
WHERE

6
BORN
WHERE
WHEN MARRIED
DIED
WHERE

7
BORN
WHERE
DIED
WHERE

8
BORN
WHERE
WHEN MARRIED
DIED
WHERE

9
BORN
WHERE
DIED
WHERE

10
BORN
WHERE
WHEN MARRIED
DIED
WHERE

11
BORN
WHERE
DIED
WHERE

12
BORN
WHERE
WHEN MARRIED
DIED
WHERE

13
BORN
WHERE
DIED
WHERE

14
BORN
WHERE
WHEN MARRIED
DIED
WHERE

15
BORN
WHERE
DIED
WHERE

16

17

18

19

20

21

22

23

24

25

26

27

28

29

30

31

SOURCES OF INFORMATION

GENEALOGICAL CHART

CHART NO. ②

Date _____

Compiler _____

Address _____

_____
City   State   Zip

NO. 1 IS THE SAME PERSON AS NO. _____ ON CHART NO. _____

NAME
CONTINUED
ON CHART

FATHER

HOSEY

2
BORN
WHERE
WHEN MARRIED
DIED
WHERE

4
BORN
WHERE
WHEN MARRIED
DIED
WHERE

5
BORN
WHERE
DIED
WHERE

8
BORN
WHERE
WHEN MARRIED
DIED
WHERE

9
BORN
WHERE
DIED
WHERE

16

17

18

19

1 **JOAN ⚹HOSEY**
BORN
WHERE
WHEN MARRIED
DIED
WHERE

NAME OF HUSBAND OR WIFE

CHART NO. _____

MOTHER
SALLY HAGGERTY

3
BORN
WHERE
DIED
WHERE **SARASOTA FL.**

10
BORN
WHERE
WHEN MARRIED
DIED
WHERE

11
BORN
WHERE
DIED
WHERE

20

21

22

23

6
BORN
WHERE
WHEN MARRIED
DIED
WHERE

7
BORN
WHERE
DIED
WHERE

12
BORN
WHERE
WHEN MARRIED
DIED
WHERE

13
BORN
WHERE
DIED
WHERE

24

25

26

27

14
BORN
WHERE
WHEN MARRIED
DIED
WHERE

15
BORN
WHERE
DIED
WHERE

28

29

30

31

SOURCES OF INFORMATION

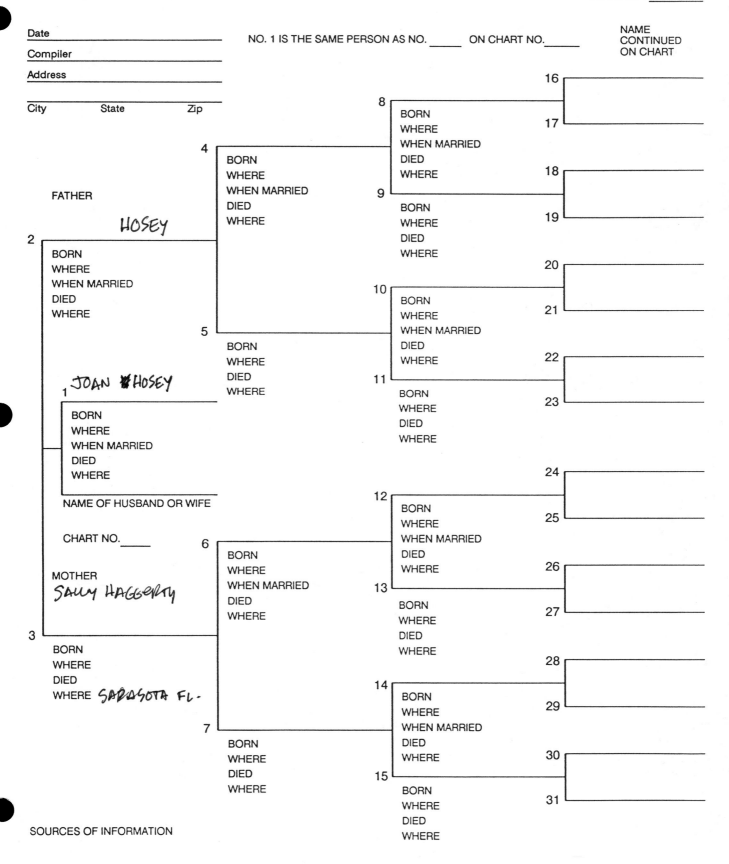

GENEALOGICAL CHART

CHART NO. _____

Date _____

Compiler _____

Address _____

_____

City   State   Zip

NO. 1 IS THE SAME PERSON AS NO. ② ON CHART NO. ①

NAME CONTINUED ON CHART

FATHER

4
BORN
WHERE
WHEN MARRIED
DIED
WHERE

8
BORN
WHERE
WHEN MARRIED
DIED
WHERE

16 _____

17 _____

2
BORN
WHERE
WHEN MARRIED
DIED
WHERE

9
BORN
WHERE
DIED
WHERE

18 _____

19 _____

5
BORN
WHERE
DIED
WHERE

10
BORN
WHERE
WHEN MARRIED
DIED
WHERE

20 _____

21 _____

1 WILLIAM BROWNE
BORN
WHERE
WHEN MARRIED
DIED
WHERE

11
BORN
WHERE
DIED
WHERE

22 _____

23 _____

NAME OF HUSBAND OR WIFE

CHART NO. _____

12
BORN
WHERE
WHEN MARRIED
DIED
WHERE

24 _____

25 _____

MOTHER

6
BORN
WHERE
WHEN MARRIED
DIED
WHERE

13
BORN
WHERE
DIED
WHERE

26 _____

27 _____

3
BORN
WHERE
DIED
WHERE

14
BORN
WHERE
WHEN MARRIED
DIED
WHERE

28 _____

29 _____

7
BORN
WHERE
DIED
WHERE

15
BORN
WHERE
DIED
WHERE

30 _____

31 _____

SOURCES OF INFORMATION

GENEALOGICAL CHART

CHART NO. _____

Date _____

Compiler _____

Address _____

_____

City   State   Zip

NO. 1 IS THE SAME PERSON AS NO. ③ ON CHART NO. ①

NAME
CONTINUED
ON CHART

FATHER

4
BORN
WHERE
WHEN MARRIED
DIED
WHERE

8
BORN
WHERE
WHEN MARRIED
DIED
WHERE

16 _____

17 _____

9
BORN
WHERE
DIED
WHERE

18 _____

19 _____

2
BORN
WHERE
WHEN MARRIED
DIED
WHERE

5
BORN
WHERE
DIED
WHERE

10
BORN
WHERE
WHEN MARRIED
DIED
WHERE

20 _____

21 _____

11
BORN
WHERE
DIED
WHERE

22 _____

23 _____

1 MAE COLLINS?
BORN
WHERE
WHEN MARRIED
DIED
WHERE

NAME OF HUSBAND OR WIFE

CHART NO. _____

MOTHER

6
BORN
WHERE
WHEN MARRIED
DIED
WHERE

12
BORN
WHERE
WHEN MARRIED
DIED
WHERE

24 _____

25 _____

13
BORN
WHERE
DIED
WHERE

26 _____

27 _____

3
BORN
WHERE
DIED
WHERE

7
BORN
WHERE
DIED
WHERE

14
BORN
WHERE
WHEN MARRIED
DIED
WHERE

28 _____

29 _____

15
BORN
WHERE
DIED
WHERE

30 _____

31 _____

SOURCES OF INFORMATION

GENEALOGICAL CHART

CHART NO. _____

Date _____

Compiler _____

Address _____

City   State   Zip

NO. 1 IS THE SAME PERSON AS NO. ② ON CHART NO. ②

NAME
CONTINUED
ON CHART

FATHER

4
BORN
WHERE
WHEN MARRIED
DIED
WHERE

2
BORN
WHERE
WHEN MARRIED
DIED
WHERE

5
BORN
WHERE
DIED
WHERE

1   HOSEY
BORN
WHERE
WHEN MARRIED
DIED
WHERE

NAME OF HUSBAND OR WIFE

CHART NO. _____

MOTHER

6
BORN
WHERE
WHEN MARRIED
DIED
WHERE

3
BORN
WHERE
DIED
WHERE

7
BORN
WHERE
DIED
WHERE

8
BORN
WHERE
WHEN MARRIED
DIED
WHERE

9
BORN
WHERE
DIED
WHERE

10
BORN
WHERE
WHEN MARRIED
DIED
WHERE

11
BORN
WHERE
DIED
WHERE

12
BORN
WHERE
WHEN MARRIED
DIED
WHERE

13
BORN
WHERE
DIED
WHERE

14
BORN
WHERE
WHEN MARRIED
DIED
WHERE

15
BORN
WHERE
DIED
WHERE

16 _____
17 _____
18 _____
19 _____
20 _____
21 _____
22 _____
23 _____
24 _____
25 _____
26 _____
27 _____
28 _____
29 _____
30 _____
31 _____

SOURCES OF INFORMATION

GENEALOGICAL CHART

CHART NO. _____

Date _____

Compiler _____

Address _____

_____
City   State   Zip

NO. 1 IS THE SAME PERSON AS NO. ③ ON CHART NO. ②

NAME
CONTINUED
ON CHART

FATHER

2
BORN
WHERE
WHEN MARRIED
DIED
WHERE

4
BORN
WHERE
WHEN MARRIED
DIED
WHERE

5
BORN
WHERE
DIED
WHERE

8
BORN
WHERE
WHEN MARRIED
DIED
WHERE

9
BORN
WHERE
DIED
WHERE

16

17

18

19

10
BORN
WHERE
WHEN MARRIED
DIED
WHERE

11
BORN
WHERE
DIED
WHERE

20

21

22

23

1 SALCY HAGGERTY
BORN
WHERE
WHEN MARRIED
DIED
WHERE

NAME OF HUSBAND OR WIFE

CHART NO. _____

MOTHER

3
BORN
WHERE
DIED
WHERE

6
BORN
WHERE
WHEN MARRIED
DIED
WHERE

7
BORN
WHERE
DIED
WHERE

12
BORN
WHERE
WHEN MARRIED
DIED
WHERE

13
BORN
WHERE
DIED
WHERE

24

25

26

27

14
BORN
WHERE
WHEN MARRIED
DIED
WHERE

15
BORN
WHERE
DIED
WHERE

28

29

30

31

SOURCES OF INFORMATION

GENEALOGICAL CHART

CHART NO. _____

Date _____

Compiler _____

Address _____

City _____ State _____ Zip _____

NO. 1 IS THE SAME PERSON AS NO. _____ ON CHART NO. _____

NAME
CONTINUED
ON CHART

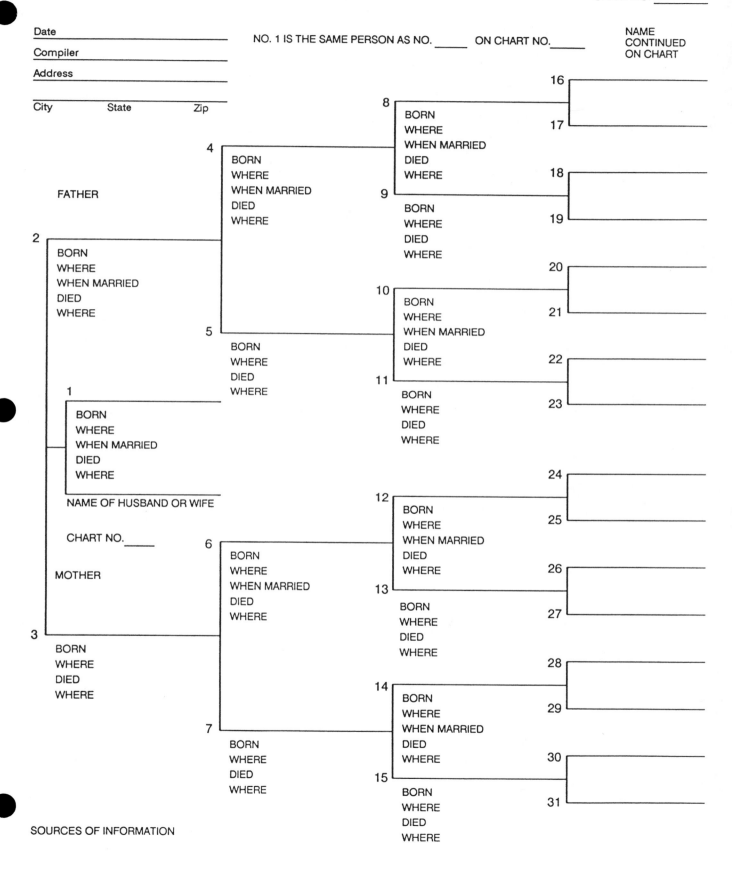

FATHER

2
BORN
WHERE
WHEN MARRIED
DIED
WHERE

4
BORN
WHERE
WHEN MARRIED
DIED
WHERE

8
BORN
WHERE
WHEN MARRIED
DIED
WHERE

16

17

9
BORN
WHERE
DIED
WHERE

18

19

5
BORN
WHERE
DIED
WHERE

10
BORN
WHERE
WHEN MARRIED
DIED
WHERE

20

21

11
BORN
WHERE
DIED
WHERE

22

23

1
BORN
WHERE
WHEN MARRIED
DIED
WHERE

NAME OF HUSBAND OR WIFE

CHART NO. _____

MOTHER

3
BORN
WHERE
DIED
WHERE

6
BORN
WHERE
WHEN MARRIED
DIED
WHERE

12
BORN
WHERE
WHEN MARRIED
DIED
WHERE

24

25

13
BORN
WHERE
DIED
WHERE

26

27

7
BORN
WHERE
DIED
WHERE

14
BORN
WHERE
WHEN MARRIED
DIED
WHERE

28

29

15
BORN
WHERE
DIED
WHERE

30

31

SOURCES OF INFORMATION

GENEALOGICAL CHART

CHART NO. _____

Date _____

NO. 1 IS THE SAME PERSON AS NO. _____ ON CHART NO. _____

NAME
CONTINUED
ON CHART

Compiler _____

Address _____

City   State   Zip

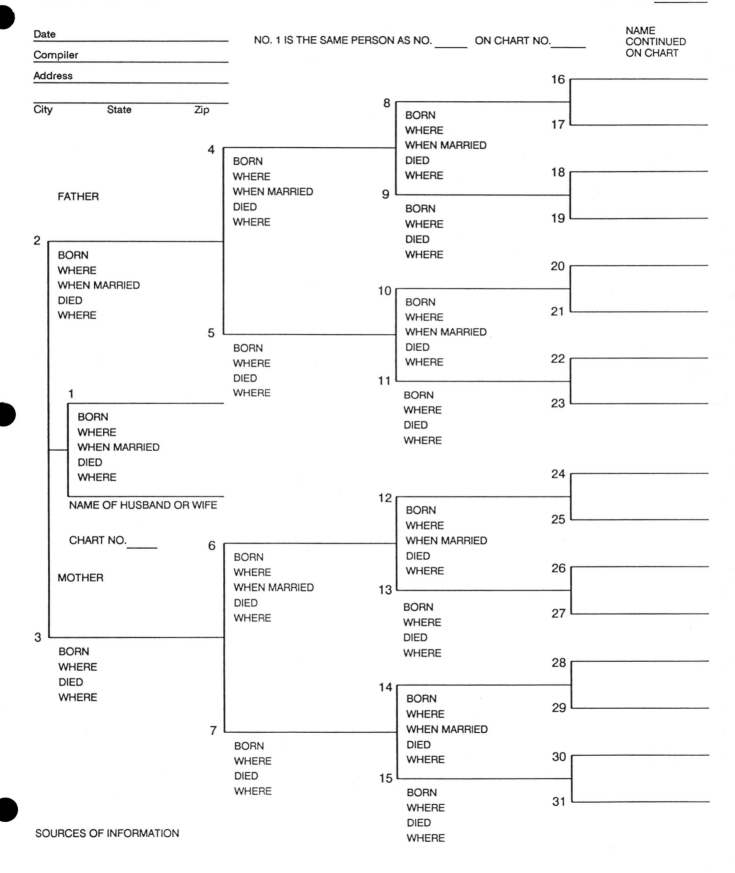

FATHER

2
BORN
WHERE
WHEN MARRIED
DIED
WHERE

4
BORN
WHERE
WHEN MARRIED
DIED
WHERE

5
BORN
WHERE
DIED
WHERE

8
BORN
WHERE
WHEN MARRIED
DIED
WHERE

16

17

9
BORN
WHERE
DIED
WHERE

18

19

10
BORN
WHERE
WHEN MARRIED
DIED
WHERE

20

21

11
BORN
WHERE
DIED
WHERE

22

23

1
BORN
WHERE
WHEN MARRIED
DIED
WHERE

NAME OF HUSBAND OR WIFE

CHART NO. _____

MOTHER

3
BORN
WHERE
DIED
WHERE

6
BORN
WHERE
WHEN MARRIED
DIED
WHERE

7
BORN
WHERE
DIED
WHERE

12
BORN
WHERE
WHEN MARRIED
DIED
WHERE

24

25

13
BORN
WHERE
DIED
WHERE

26

27

14
BORN
WHERE
WHEN MARRIED
DIED
WHERE

28

29

15
BORN
WHERE
DIED
WHERE

30

31

SOURCES OF INFORMATION

GENEALOGICAL CHART

CHART NO. _____

Date _____

Compiler _____

Address _____

_____

City   State   Zip

NO. 1 IS THE SAME PERSON AS NO. _____ ON CHART NO. _____

NAME
CONTINUED
ON CHART

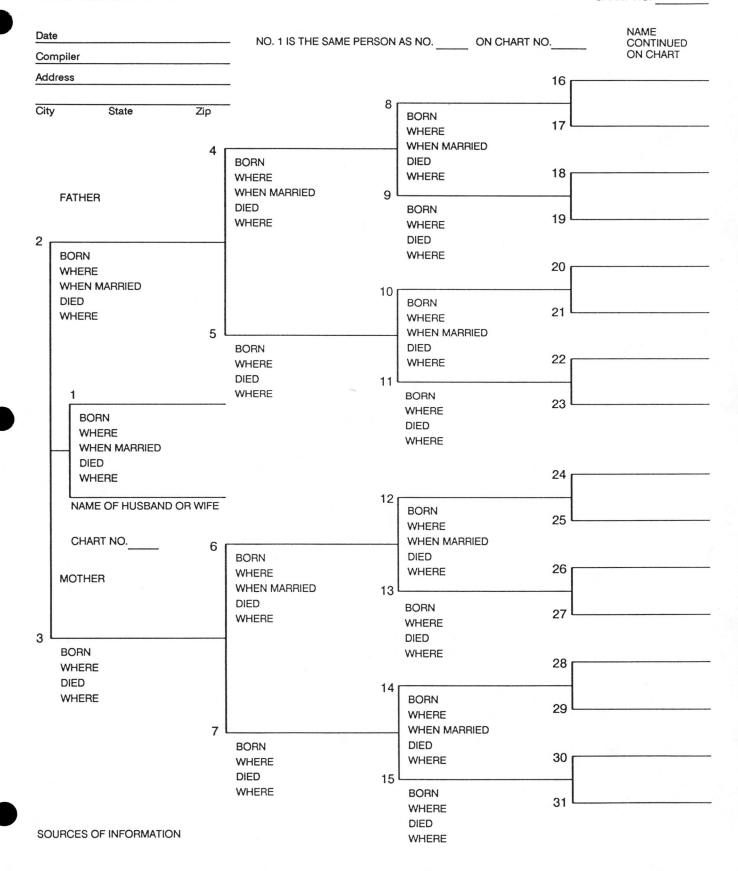

8
BORN
WHERE
WHEN MARRIED
DIED
WHERE

4
BORN
WHERE
WHEN MARRIED
DIED
WHERE

FATHER

9
BORN
WHERE
DIED
WHERE

2
BORN
WHERE
WHEN MARRIED
DIED
WHERE

16

17

18

19

5
BORN
WHERE
DIED
WHERE

10
BORN
WHERE
WHEN MARRIED
DIED
WHERE

20

21

22

11
BORN
WHERE
DIED
WHERE

23

1
BORN
WHERE
WHEN MARRIED
DIED
WHERE

NAME OF HUSBAND OR WIFE

CHART NO. _____

MOTHER

6
BORN
WHERE
WHEN MARRIED
DIED
WHERE

12
BORN
WHERE
WHEN MARRIED
DIED
WHERE

24

25

26

13
BORN
WHERE
DIED
WHERE

27

3
BORN
WHERE
DIED
WHERE

7
BORN
WHERE
DIED
WHERE

14
BORN
WHERE
WHEN MARRIED
DIED
WHERE

28

29

30

15
BORN
WHERE
DIED
WHERE

31

SOURCES OF INFORMATION

GENEALOGICAL CHART

CHART NO. _____

Date _____

Compiler _____

Address _____

_____
City   State   Zip

NO. 1 IS THE SAME PERSON AS NO. _____ ON CHART NO._____

NAME
CONTINUED
ON CHART

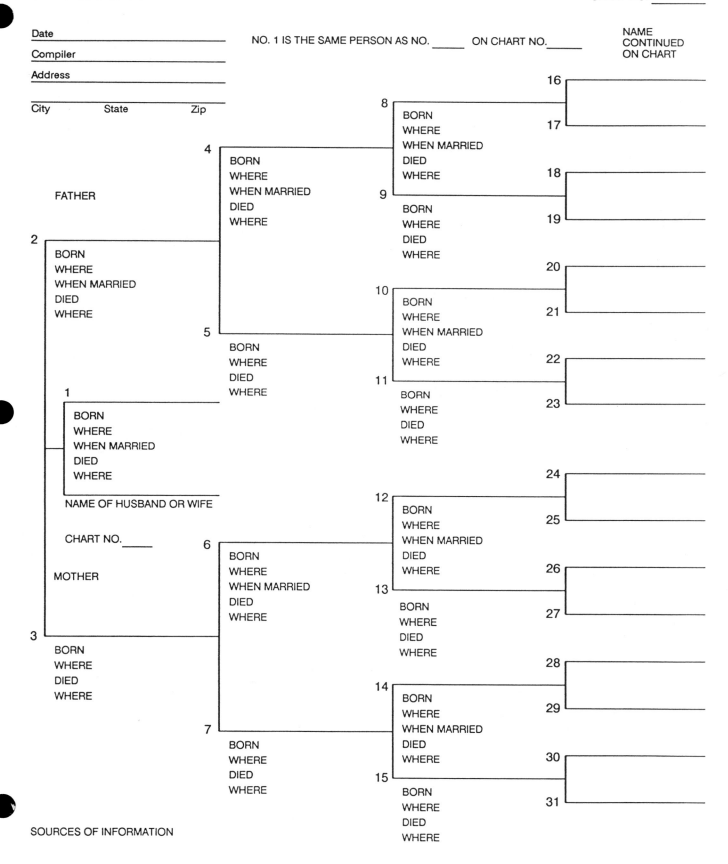

4
BORN
WHERE
WHEN MARRIED
DIED
WHERE

FATHER

2
BORN
WHERE
WHEN MARRIED
DIED
WHERE

5
BORN
WHERE
DIED
WHERE

1
BORN
WHERE
WHEN MARRIED
DIED
WHERE

NAME OF HUSBAND OR WIFE

CHART NO. _____

MOTHER

6
BORN
WHERE
WHEN MARRIED
DIED
WHERE

3
BORN
WHERE
DIED
WHERE

7
BORN
WHERE
DIED
WHERE

8
BORN
WHERE
WHEN MARRIED
DIED
WHERE

9
BORN
WHERE
DIED
WHERE

10
BORN
WHERE
WHEN MARRIED
DIED
WHERE

11
BORN
WHERE
DIED
WHERE

12
BORN
WHERE
WHEN MARRIED
DIED
WHERE

13
BORN
WHERE
DIED
WHERE

14
BORN
WHERE
WHEN MARRIED
DIED
WHERE

15
BORN
WHERE
DIED
WHERE

16
17
18
19
20
21
22
23
24
25
26
27
28
29
30
31

SOURCES OF INFORMATION

GENEALOGICAL CHART

CHART NO. _____

Date _____

Compiler _____

Address _____

City   State   Zip

NO. 1 IS THE SAME PERSON AS NO. _____ ON CHART NO. _____

NAME
CONTINUED
ON CHART

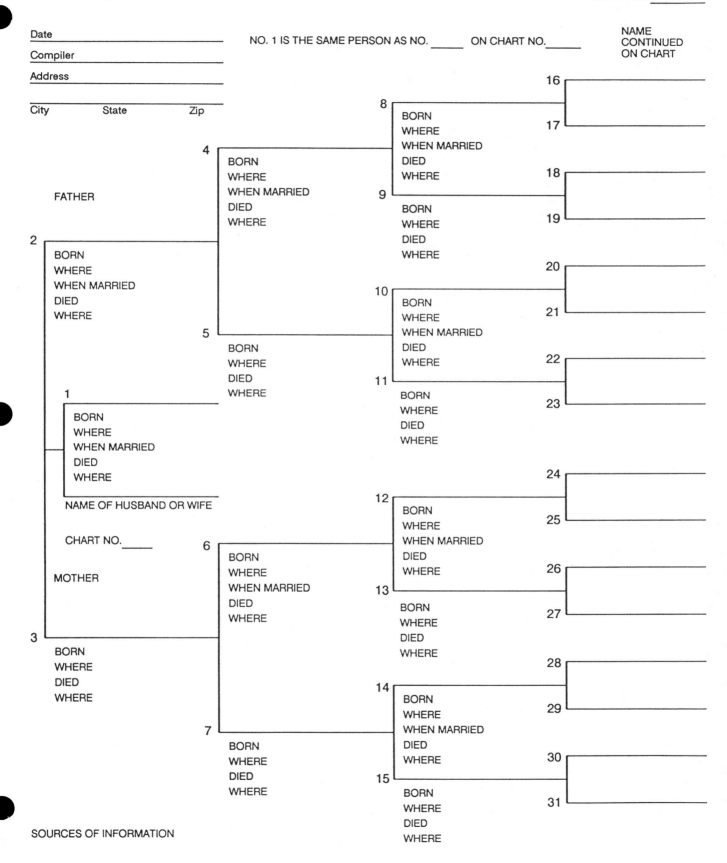

4

BORN
WHERE
WHEN MARRIED
DIED
WHERE

FATHER

2

BORN
WHERE
WHEN MARRIED
DIED
WHERE

5

BORN
WHERE
DIED
WHERE

1

BORN
WHERE
WHEN MARRIED
DIED
WHERE

NAME OF HUSBAND OR WIFE

CHART NO. _____

MOTHER

3

BORN
WHERE
DIED
WHERE

6

BORN
WHERE
WHEN MARRIED
DIED
WHERE

7

BORN
WHERE
DIED
WHERE

8

BORN
WHERE
WHEN MARRIED
DIED
WHERE

9

BORN
WHERE
DIED
WHERE

10

BORN
WHERE
WHEN MARRIED
DIED
WHERE

11

BORN
WHERE
DIED
WHERE

12

BORN
WHERE
WHEN MARRIED
DIED
WHERE

13

BORN
WHERE
DIED
WHERE

14

BORN
WHERE
WHEN MARRIED
DIED
WHERE

15

BORN
WHERE
DIED
WHERE

16

17

18

19

20

21

22

23

24

25

26

27

28

29

30

31

SOURCES OF INFORMATION

GENEALOGICAL CHART

CHART NO. _____

Date _____

Compiler _____

Address _____

City   State   Zip

NO. 1 IS THE SAME PERSON AS NO. _____ ON CHART NO. _____

NAME
CONTINUED
ON CHART

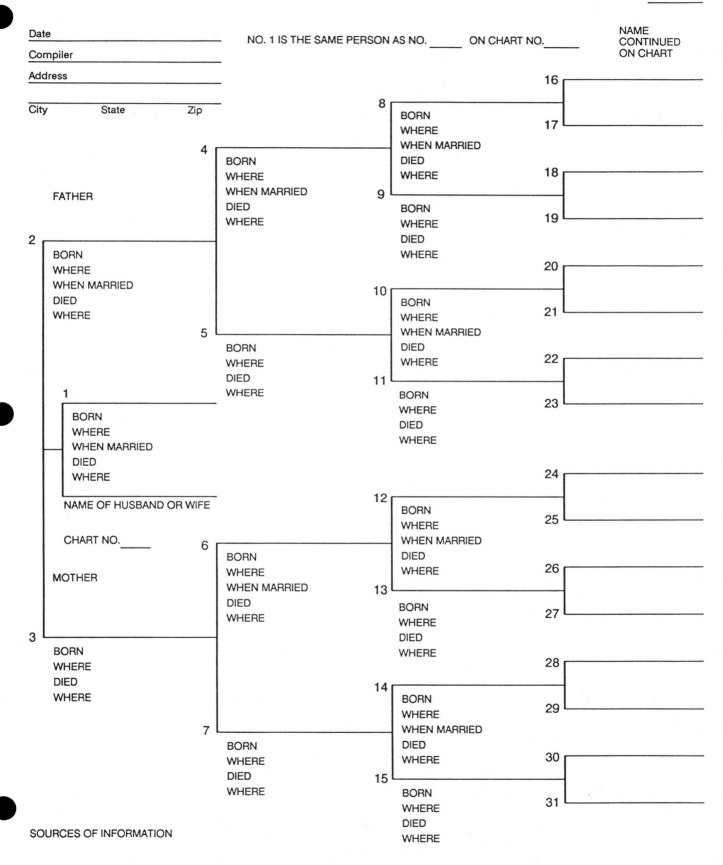

FATHER

2
BORN
WHERE
WHEN MARRIED
DIED
WHERE

1
BORN
WHERE
WHEN MARRIED
DIED
WHERE

NAME OF HUSBAND OR WIFE

CHART NO. _____

MOTHER

3
BORN
WHERE
DIED
WHERE

4
BORN
WHERE
WHEN MARRIED
DIED
WHERE

5
BORN
WHERE
DIED
WHERE

6
BORN
WHERE
WHEN MARRIED
DIED
WHERE

7
BORN
WHERE
DIED
WHERE

8
BORN
WHERE
WHEN MARRIED
DIED
WHERE

9
BORN
WHERE
DIED
WHERE

10
BORN
WHERE
WHEN MARRIED
DIED
WHERE

11
BORN
WHERE
DIED
WHERE

12
BORN
WHERE
WHEN MARRIED
DIED
WHERE

13
BORN
WHERE
DIED
WHERE

14
BORN
WHERE
WHEN MARRIED
DIED
WHERE

15
BORN
WHERE
DIED
WHERE

16
17
18
19
20
21
22
23
24
25
26
27
28
29
30
31

SOURCES OF INFORMATION

GENEALOGICAL CHART

CHART NO. _____

Date _____

Compiler _____

Address _____

City   State   Zip

NO. 1 IS THE SAME PERSON AS NO. _____ ON CHART NO. _____

NAME
CONTINUED
ON CHART

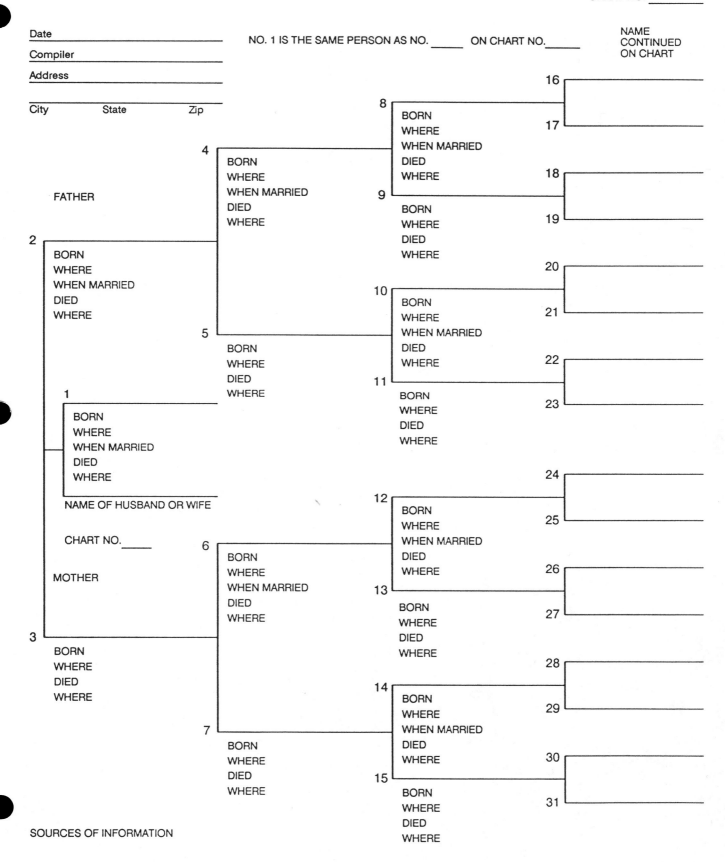

FATHER

2
BORN
WHERE
WHEN MARRIED
DIED
WHERE

1
BORN
WHERE
WHEN MARRIED
DIED
WHERE

NAME OF HUSBAND OR WIFE

CHART NO. _____

MOTHER

3
BORN
WHERE
DIED
WHERE

4
BORN
WHERE
WHEN MARRIED
DIED
WHERE

5
BORN
WHERE
DIED
WHERE

6
BORN
WHERE
WHEN MARRIED
DIED
WHERE

7
BORN
WHERE
DIED
WHERE

8
BORN
WHERE
WHEN MARRIED
DIED
WHERE

9
BORN
WHERE
DIED
WHERE

10
BORN
WHERE
WHEN MARRIED
DIED
WHERE

11
BORN
WHERE
DIED
WHERE

12
BORN
WHERE
WHEN MARRIED
DIED
WHERE

13
BORN
WHERE
DIED
WHERE

14
BORN
WHERE
WHEN MARRIED
DIED
WHERE

15
BORN
WHERE
DIED
WHERE

16

17

18

19

20

21

22

23

24

25

26

27

28

29

30

31

SOURCES OF INFORMATION

GENEALOGICAL CHART

CHART NO. _____

Date _____

Compiler _____

Address _____

City   State   Zip

NO. 1 IS THE SAME PERSON AS NO. _____ ON CHART NO._____

NAME
CONTINUED
ON CHART

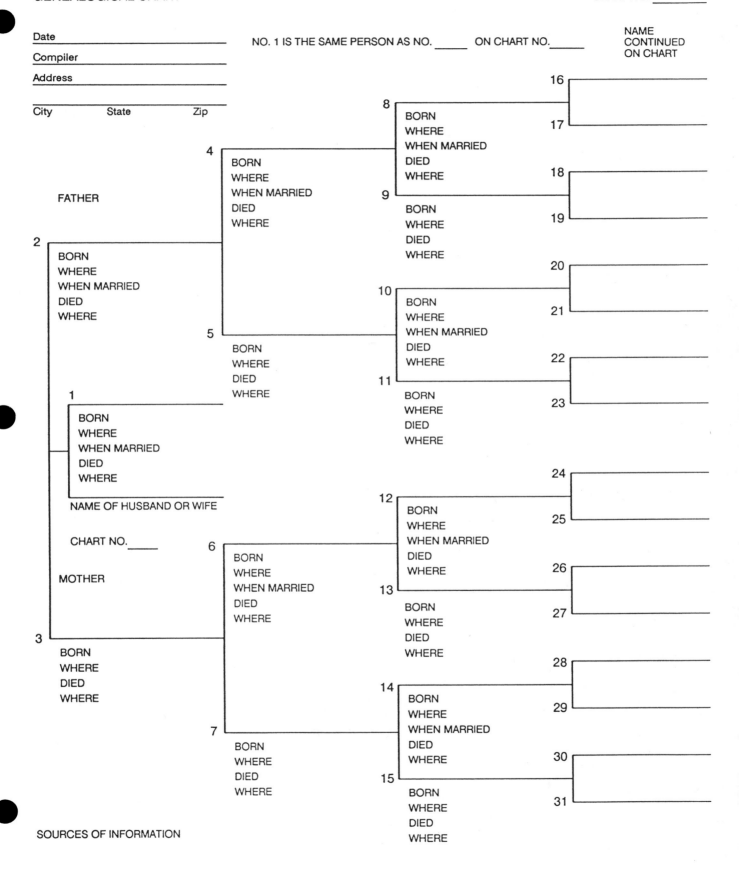

FATHER

2
BORN
WHERE
WHEN MARRIED
DIED
WHERE

4
BORN
WHERE
WHEN MARRIED
DIED
WHERE

8
BORN
WHERE
WHEN MARRIED
DIED
WHERE

16 _____

17 _____

9
BORN
WHERE
DIED
WHERE

18 _____

19 _____

5
BORN
WHERE
DIED
WHERE

10
BORN
WHERE
WHEN MARRIED
DIED
WHERE

20 _____

21 _____

11
BORN
WHERE
DIED
WHERE

22 _____

23 _____

1
BORN
WHERE
WHEN MARRIED
DIED
WHERE

NAME OF HUSBAND OR WIFE

CHART NO._____

MOTHER

3
BORN
WHERE
DIED
WHERE

6
BORN
WHERE
WHEN MARRIED
DIED
WHERE

12
BORN
WHERE
WHEN MARRIED
DIED
WHERE

24 _____

25 _____

13
BORN
WHERE
DIED
WHERE

26 _____

27 _____

7
BORN
WHERE
DIED
WHERE

14
BORN
WHERE
WHEN MARRIED
DIED
WHERE

28 _____

29 _____

15
BORN
WHERE
DIED
WHERE

30 _____

31 _____

SOURCES OF INFORMATION

GENEALOGICAL CHART

CHART NO. _____

Date _____

Compiler _____

Address _____

_____

City   State   Zip

NO. 1 IS THE SAME PERSON AS NO. _____ ON CHART NO. _____

NAME
CONTINUED
ON CHART

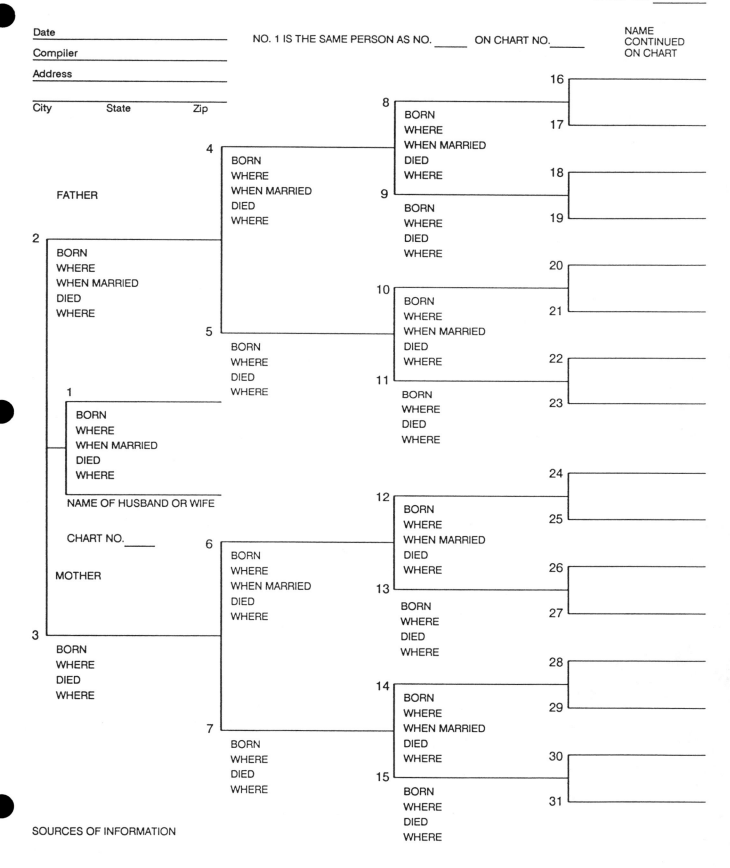

4
BORN
WHERE
WHEN MARRIED
DIED
WHERE

FATHER

2
BORN
WHERE
WHEN MARRIED
DIED
WHERE

5
BORN
WHERE
DIED
WHERE

1
BORN
WHERE
WHEN MARRIED
DIED
WHERE

NAME OF HUSBAND OR WIFE

CHART NO._____

MOTHER

3
BORN
WHERE
DIED
WHERE

6
BORN
WHERE
WHEN MARRIED
DIED
WHERE

7
BORN
WHERE
DIED
WHERE

8
BORN
WHERE
WHEN MARRIED
DIED
WHERE

9
BORN
WHERE
DIED
WHERE

10
BORN
WHERE
WHEN MARRIED
DIED
WHERE

11
BORN
WHERE
DIED
WHERE

12
BORN
WHERE
WHEN MARRIED
DIED
WHERE

13
BORN
WHERE
DIED
WHERE

14
BORN
WHERE
WHEN MARRIED
DIED
WHERE

15
BORN
WHERE
DIED
WHERE

16
17
18
19
20
21
22
23
24
25
26
27
28
29
30
31

SOURCES OF INFORMATION

GENEALOGICAL CHART

CHART NO. _____

Date _____

Compiler _____

Address _____

_____
City   State   Zip

NO. 1 IS THE SAME PERSON AS NO. _____ ON CHART NO. _____

NAME
CONTINUED
ON CHART

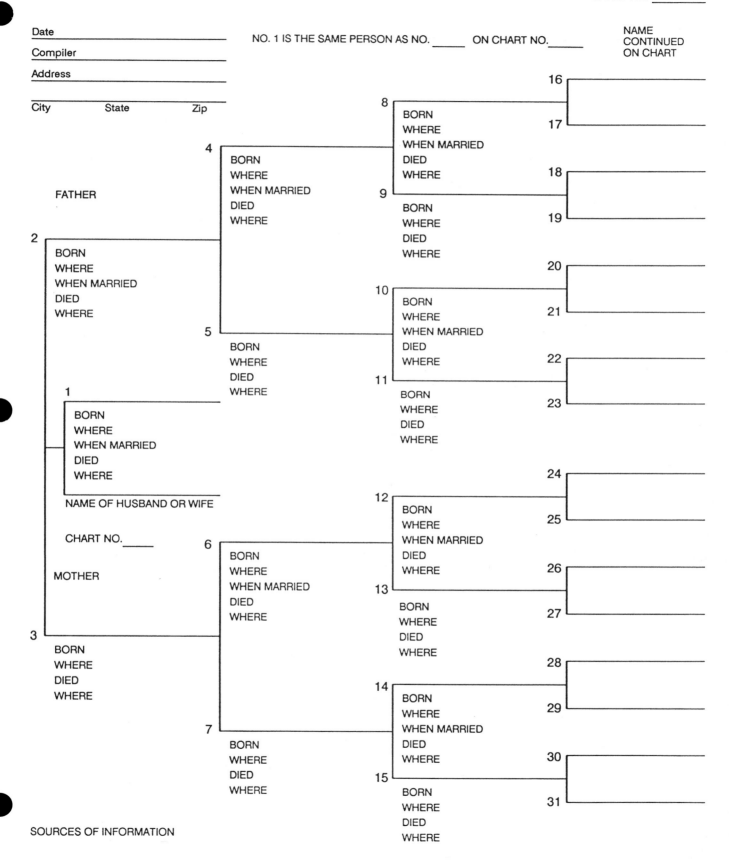

16

8
BORN
WHERE
WHEN MARRIED
DIED
WHERE

17

4
BORN
WHERE
WHEN MARRIED
DIED
WHERE

FATHER

18

9
BORN
WHERE
DIED
WHERE

19

2
BORN
WHERE
WHEN MARRIED
DIED
WHERE

20

10
BORN
WHERE
WHEN MARRIED
DIED
WHERE

21

5
BORN
WHERE
DIED
WHERE

22

11
BORN
WHERE
DIED
WHERE

23

1
BORN
WHERE
WHEN MARRIED
DIED
WHERE

NAME OF HUSBAND OR WIFE

CHART NO. _____

24

12
BORN
WHERE
WHEN MARRIED
DIED
WHERE

25

MOTHER

6
BORN
WHERE
WHEN MARRIED
DIED
WHERE

26

13
BORN
WHERE
DIED
WHERE

27

3
BORN
WHERE
DIED
WHERE

28

14
BORN
WHERE
WHEN MARRIED
DIED
WHERE

29

7
BORN
WHERE
DIED
WHERE

30

15
BORN
WHERE
DIED
WHERE

31

SOURCES OF INFORMATION

ANCESTOR CHART

SURNAME **BROWNE**

HUSBAND	RICHARD ARTHUR ALAN — THE SAME PERSON AS NO. ① ON CHART ①
BORN	NEW YORK - AUG. 11, 1917
WHERE	NEW YORK,
WHEN MARRIED	WHERE
DIED	JUNE 4, 1989
WHERE	SARASOTA FL.
HUSBAND'S FATHER	WILLIAM CHART NO. MOTHER MAE CHART NO.
HUSBAND'S OTHER WIVES	

WIFE	Maiden Name JOAN MARIE HOSEY THE SAME PERSON AS NO. ① ON CHART ②
BORN	~~New York~~
WHERE	
DIED	~~SARASOTA FL.~~ 1986
WHERE	SARASOTA, FL.
WIFE'S FATHER	HOSEY CHART NO. MOTHER SALLY HAGGERTY CHART NO.
WIFE'S OTHER HUSBANDS	

Child	Sex	CHILDREN of this marriage	BORN Date	Place	DIED Date	Place	MARRIED TO Date	Place
1	M	ROBERT DAVID	~~JUNE~~ 17, 1948 · NY JULY ?				DEBORAH KASCOVE SARASOTA, FL.	
2	M	CHRISTOPHER KELLY	MAY 16, 1952 NJ E. ~~SOUTH~~ ORANGE,				CARROLL SMITH SARASOTA. MAR 10, 1989.	
3 (ADOPTED)	F	SALLY ANN (AKA: TSUI MAN WONG)	HONG KONG				WERNER FAGERER WASHINGTON DC.	
4								
5								
6								
7								
8								
9								
10								
11								
12								

SOURCES OF INFORMATION
or documentation

Date JUNE 17, 1995
Compiler *Chris Browne* CHRIS BROWNE
Address 531 REID ST.
SARASOTA FL 34242
City   State   Zip

ANCESTOR CHART

SURNAME _____

HUSBAND _____ THE SAME PERSON AS NO. _____ ON CHART _____
BORN _____
WHERE _____
WHEN MARRIED _____ WHERE _____
DIED _____
WHERE _____
HUSBAND'S   FATHER _____ CHART NO. _____ MOTHER _____ CHART NO. _____
HUSBAND'S OTHER WIVES _____

WIFE   Maiden Name _____ THE SAME PERSON AS NO. _____ ON CHART _____
BORN _____
WHERE _____
DIED _____
WHERE _____
WIFE'S   FATHER _____ CHART NO. _____ MOTHER _____ CHART NO. _____
WIFE'S OTHER HUSBANDS _____

Child	Sex	CHILDREN of this marriage	BORN Date	Place	DIED Date	Place	MARRIED TO Date	Place
1								
2								
3								
4								
5								
6								
7								
8								
9								
10								
11								
12								

SOURCES OF INFORMATION
or documentation

Date _____

Compiler _____

Address _____

_____
City   State   Zip

ANCESTOR CHART

SURNAME _____

HUSBAND _____ THE SAME PERSON AS NO. _____ ON CHART _____
BORN _____
WHERE _____
WHEN MARRIED _____ WHERE _____
DIED _____
WHERE _____
HUSBAND'S FATHER _____ CHART NO. _____ MOTHER _____ CHART NO. _____
HUSBAND'S OTHER WIVES _____

WIFE Maiden Name _____ THE SAME PERSON AS NO. _____ ON CHART _____
BORN _____
WHERE _____
DIED _____
WHERE _____
WIFE'S FATHER _____ CHART NO. _____ MOTHER _____ CHART NO. _____
WIFE'S OTHER HUSBANDS _____

Child	Sex	CHILDREN of this marriage	BORN Date	Place	DIED Date	Place	MARRIED TO Date	Place
1								
2								
3								
4								
5								
6								
7								
8								
9								
10								
11								
12								

SOURCES OF INFORMATION
or documentation

Date _____

Compiler _____

Address _____

City _____ State _____ Zip _____

ANCESTOR CHART

SURNAME _____

HUSBAND _____ THE SAME PERSON AS NO. _____ ON CHART _____
BORN _____
WHERE _____
WHEN MARRIED _____ WHERE _____
DIED _____
WHERE _____
HUSBAND'S FATHER _____ CHART NO. _____ MOTHER _____ CHART NO. _____
HUSBAND'S OTHER WIVES _____

WIFE Maiden Name _____ THE SAME PERSON AS NO. _____ ON CHART _____
BORN _____
WHERE _____
DIED _____
WHERE _____
WIFE'S FATHER _____ CHART NO. _____ MOTHER _____ CHART NO. _____
WIFE'S OTHER HUSBANDS _____

Child	Sex	CHILDREN of this marriage	BORN Date	Place	DIED Date	Place	MARRIED TO Date	Place
1								
2								
3								
4								
5								
6								
7								
8								
9								
10								
11								
12								

SOURCES OF INFORMATION
or documentation

Date _____
Compiler _____
Address _____

City _____ State _____ Zip _____

ANCESTOR CHART

SURNAME _____

HUSBAND _____ THE SAME PERSON AS NO. _____ ON CHART _____
BORN _____
WHERE _____
WHEN MARRIED _____ WHERE _____
DIED _____
WHERE _____
HUSBAND'S FATHER _____ CHART NO. _____ MOTHER _____ CHART NO. _____
HUSBAND'S OTHER WIVES _____

WIFE _____ Maiden Name _____ THE SAME PERSON AS NO. _____ ON CHART _____
BORN _____
WHERE _____
DIED _____
WHERE _____
WIFE'S FATHER _____ CHART NO. _____ MOTHER _____ CHART NO. _____
WIFE'S OTHER HUSBANDS _____

Child	Sex	CHILDREN of this marriage	BORN Date	Place	DIED Date	Place	MARRIED TO Date	Place
1								
2								
3								
4								
5								
6								
7								
8								
9								
10								
11								
12								

SOURCES OF INFORMATION
or documentation

Date _____

Compiler _____

Address _____

City _____ State _____ Zip _____

ANCESTOR CHART

SURNAME _____

HUSBAND _____ THE SAME PERSON AS NO. _____ ON CHART _____
BORN _____
WHERE _____
WHEN MARRIED _____ WHERE _____
DIED _____
WHERE _____
HUSBAND'S FATHER _____ CHART NO. _____ MOTHER _____ CHART NO. _____
HUSBAND'S OTHER WIVES _____

WIFE Maiden Name _____ THE SAME PERSON AS NO. _____ ON CHART _____
BORN _____
WHERE _____
DIED _____
WHERE _____
WIFE'S FATHER _____ CHART NO. _____ MOTHER _____ CHART NO. _____
WIFE'S OTHER HUSBANDS _____

Child	Sex	CHILDREN of this marriage	BORN Date	Place	DIED Date	Place	MARRIED TO Date	Place
1								
2								
3								
4								
5								
6								
7								
8								
9								
10								
11								
12								

SOURCES OF INFORMATION
or documentation

Date _____
Compiler _____
Address _____

City _____ State _____ Zip _____

ANCESTOR CHART

SURNAME _____

HUSBAND _____ THE SAME PERSON AS NO. _____ ON CHART _____
BORN _____
WHERE _____
WHEN MARRIED _____ WHERE _____
DIED _____
WHERE _____
HUSBAND'S FATHER _____ CHART NO. _____ MOTHER _____ CHART NO. _____
HUSBAND'S OTHER WIVES _____

WIFE Maiden Name _____ THE SAME PERSON AS NO. _____ ON CHART _____
BORN _____
WHERE _____
DIED _____
WHERE _____
WIFE'S FATHER _____ CHART NO. _____ MOTHER _____ CHART NO. _____
WIFE'S OTHER HUSBANDS _____

Child	Sex	CHILDREN of this marriage	BORN Date	Place	DIED Date	Place	MARRIED TO Date	Place
1								
2								
3								
4								
5								
6								
7								
8								
9								
10								
11								
12								

SOURCES OF INFORMATION
or documentation

Date _____

Compiler _____

Address _____

City _____ State _____ Zip _____

ANCESTOR CHART

SURNAME _____

HUSBAND _____ THE SAME PERSON AS NO. _____ ON CHART _____
BORN _____
WHERE _____
WHEN MARRIED _____ WHERE _____
DIED _____
WHERE _____
HUSBAND'S FATHER _____ CHART NO. _____ MOTHER _____ CHART NO. _____
HUSBAND'S OTHER WIVES _____

WIFE Maiden Name _____ THE SAME PERSON AS NO. _____ ON CHART _____
BORN _____
WHERE _____
DIED _____
WHERE _____
WIFE'S FATHER _____ CHART NO. _____ MOTHER _____ CHART NO. _____
WIFE'S OTHER HUSBANDS _____

Child	Sex	CHILDREN of this marriage	BORN Date	Place	DIED Date	Place	MARRIED TO Date	Place
1								
2								
3								
4								
5								
6								
7								
8								
9								
10								
11								
12								

SOURCES OF INFORMATION
or documentation

Date _____
Compiler _____
Address _____

City _____ State _____ Zip _____

ANCESTOR CHART

SURNAME _____

HUSBAND _____ THE SAME PERSON AS NO. _____ ON CHART _____
BORN _____
WHERE _____
WHEN MARRIED _____ WHERE _____
DIED _____
WHERE _____
HUSBAND'S FATHER _____ CHART NO. _____ MOTHER _____ CHART NO. _____
HUSBAND'S OTHER WIVES _____

WIFE Maiden Name _____ THE SAME PERSON AS NO. _____ ON CHART _____
BORN _____
WHERE _____
DIED _____
WHERE _____
WIFE'S FATHER _____ CHART NO. _____ MOTHER _____ CHART NO. _____
WIFE'S OTHER HUSBANDS _____

Child	Sex	CHILDREN of this marriage	BORN Date	Place	DIED Date	Place	MARRIED TO Date	Place
1								
2								
3								
4								
5								
6								
7								
8								
9								
10								
11								
12								

SOURCES OF INFORMATION
or documentation

Date _____
Compiler _____
Address _____
_____
City   State   Zip

ANCESTOR CHART

SURNAME _____

HUSBAND _____ THE SAME PERSON AS NO. _____ ON CHART _____
BORN _____
WHERE _____
WHEN MARRIED _____ WHERE _____
DIED _____
WHERE _____
HUSBAND'S FATHER _____ CHART NO. _____ MOTHER _____ CHART NO. _____
HUSBAND'S OTHER WIVES _____

WIFE Maiden Name _____ THE SAME PERSON AS NO. _____ ON CHART _____
BORN _____
WHERE _____
DIED _____
WHERE _____
WIFE'S FATHER _____ CHART NO. _____ MOTHER _____ CHART NO. _____
WIFE'S OTHER HUSBANDS _____

Child	Sex	CHILDREN of this marriage	BORN		DIED		MARRIED TO	
			Date	Place	Date	Place	Date	Place
1								
2								
3								
4								
5								
6								
7								
8								
9								
10								
11								
12								

SOURCES OF INFORMATION
or documentation

Date _____

Compiler _____

Address _____

City _____ State _____ Zip _____

ANCESTOR CHART   SURNAME _____

HUSBAND _____ THE SAME PERSON AS NO. _____ ON CHART _____
BORN _____
WHERE _____
WHEN MARRIED _____ WHERE _____
DIED _____
WHERE _____
HUSBAND'S   FATHER _____ CHART NO. _____ MOTHER _____ CHART NO. _____
HUSBAND'S OTHER WIVES

WIFE   Maiden Name _____ THE SAME PERSON AS NO. _____ ON CHART _____
BORN _____
WHERE _____
DIED _____
WHERE _____
WIFE'S   FATHER _____ CHART NO. _____ MOTHER _____ CHART NO. _____
WIFE'S OTHER HUSBANDS

Child	Sex	CHILDREN of this marriage	BORN Date	Place	DIED Date	Place	MARRIED TO Date	Place
1								
2								
3								
4								
5								
6								
7								
8								
9								
10								
11								
12								

SOURCES OF INFORMATION
or documentation

Date _____
Compiler _____
Address _____

City _____ State _____ Zip _____

ANCESTOR CHART

SURNAME _____

HUSBAND _____ THE SAME PERSON AS NO. _____ ON CHART _____
BORN _____
WHERE _____
WHEN MARRIED _____ WHERE _____
DIED _____
WHERE _____
HUSBAND'S FATHER _____ CHART NO. _____ MOTHER _____ CHART NO. _____
HUSBAND'S OTHER WIVES _____

WIFE _____ Maiden Name _____ THE SAME PERSON AS NO. _____ ON CHART _____
BORN _____
WHERE _____
DIED _____
WHERE _____
WIFE'S FATHER _____ CHART NO. _____ MOTHER _____ CHART NO. _____
WIFE'S OTHER HUSBANDS _____

Child	Sex	CHILDREN of this marriage	BORN Date	Place	DIED Date	Place	MARRIED TO Date	Place
1								
2								
3								
4								
5								
6								
7								
8								
9								
10								
11								
12								

SOURCES OF INFORMATION
or documentation

Date _____
Compiler _____
Address _____
_____
City _____ State _____ Zip _____

ANCESTOR CHART

SURNAME _____

HUSBAND _____ THE SAME PERSON AS NO. _____ ON CHART _____
BORN _____
WHERE _____
WHEN MARRIED _____ WHERE _____
DIED _____
WHERE _____
HUSBAND'S FATHER _____ CHART NO. _____ MOTHER _____ CHART NO. _____
HUSBAND'S OTHER WIVES _____

WIFE Maiden Name _____ THE SAME PERSON AS NO. _____ ON CHART _____
BORN _____
WHERE _____
DIED _____
WHERE _____
WIFE'S FATHER _____ CHART NO. _____ MOTHER _____ CHART NO. _____
WIFE'S OTHER HUSBANDS _____

Child	Sex	CHILDREN of this marriage	BORN Date	Place	DIED Date	Place	MARRIED TO Date	Place
1								
2								
3								
4								
5								
6								
7								
8								
9								
10								
11								
12								

SOURCES OF INFORMATION
or documentation

Date _____

Compiler _____

Address _____

_____
City   State   Zip

ANCESTOR CHART

SURNAME _____

HUSBAND _____ THE SAME PERSON AS NO. _____ ON CHART _____
BORN _____
WHERE _____
WHEN MARRIED _____ WHERE _____
DIED _____
WHERE _____
HUSBAND'S FATHER _____ CHART NO. _____ MOTHER _____ CHART NO. _____
HUSBAND'S OTHER WIVES _____

WIFE Maiden Name _____ THE SAME PERSON AS NO. _____ ON CHART _____
BORN _____
WHERE _____
DIED _____
WHERE _____
WIFE'S FATHER _____ CHART NO. _____ MOTHER _____ CHART NO. _____
WIFE'S OTHER HUSBANDS _____

Child	Sex	CHILDREN of this marriage	BORN Date	Place	DIED Date	Place	MARRIED TO Date	Place
1								
2								
3								
4								
5								
6								
7								
8								
9								
10								
11								
12								

SOURCES OF INFORMATION
or documentation

Date _____
Compiler _____
Address _____

City _____ State _____ Zip _____

ANCESTOR CHART

SURNAME _____

HUSBAND _____ THE SAME PERSON AS NO. _____ ON CHART _____
BORN _____
WHERE _____
WHEN MARRIED _____ WHERE _____
DIED _____
WHERE _____
HUSBAND'S FATHER _____ CHART NO. _____ MOTHER _____ CHART NO. _____
HUSBAND'S OTHER WIVES _____

WIFE _____ Maiden Name _____ THE SAME PERSON AS NO. _____ ON CHART _____
BORN _____
WHERE _____
DIED _____
WHERE _____
WIFE'S FATHER _____ CHART NO. _____ MOTHER _____ CHART NO. _____
WIFE'S OTHER HUSBANDS _____

Child	Sex	CHILDREN of this marriage	BORN Date	Place	DIED Date	Place	MARRIED TO Date	Place
1								
2								
3								
4								
5								
6								
7								
8								
9								
10								
11								
12								

SOURCES OF INFORMATION
or documentation

Date _____

Compiler _____

Address _____

_____
City   State   Zip

ANCESTOR CHART

SURNAME _____

HUSBAND _____ THE SAME PERSON AS NO. _____ ON CHART _____
BORN _____
WHERE _____
WHEN MARRIED _____ WHERE _____
DIED _____
WHERE _____
HUSBAND'S FATHER _____ CHART NO. _____ MOTHER _____ CHART NO. _____
HUSBAND'S OTHER WIVES _____

WIFE Maiden Name _____ THE SAME PERSON AS NO. _____ ON CHART _____
BORN _____
WHERE _____
DIED _____
WHERE _____
WIFE'S FATHER _____ CHART NO. _____ MOTHER _____ CHART NO. _____
WIFE'S OTHER HUSBANDS _____

Child	Sex	CHILDREN of this marriage	BORN Date	Place	DIED Date	Place	MARRIED TO Date	Place
1								
2								
3								
4								
5								
6								
7								
8								
9								
10								
11								
12								

SOURCES OF INFORMATION
or documentation

Date _____
Compiler _____
Address _____
City _____ State _____ Zip _____

ANCESTOR CHART

SURNAME _____

HUSBAND _____   THE SAME PERSON AS NO. _____   ON CHART _____
BORN _____
WHERE _____
WHEN MARRIED _____   WHERE _____
DIED _____
WHERE _____
HUSBAND'S   FATHER _____   CHART NO. _____   MOTHER _____   CHART NO. _____
HUSBAND'S OTHER WIVES

WIFE   Maiden Name _____   THE SAME PERSON AS NO. _____   ON CHART _____
BORN _____
WHERE _____
DIED _____
WHERE _____
WIFE'S   FATHER _____   CHART NO. _____   MOTHER _____   CHART NO. _____
WIFE'S OTHER HUSBANDS

Child	Sex	CHILDREN of this marriage	BORN Date	Place	DIED Date	Place	MARRIED TO Date	Place
1								
2								
3								
4								
5								
6								
7								
8								
9								
10								
11								
12								

SOURCES OF INFORMATION
or documentation

Date _____

Compiler _____

Address _____

City _____   State _____   Zip _____